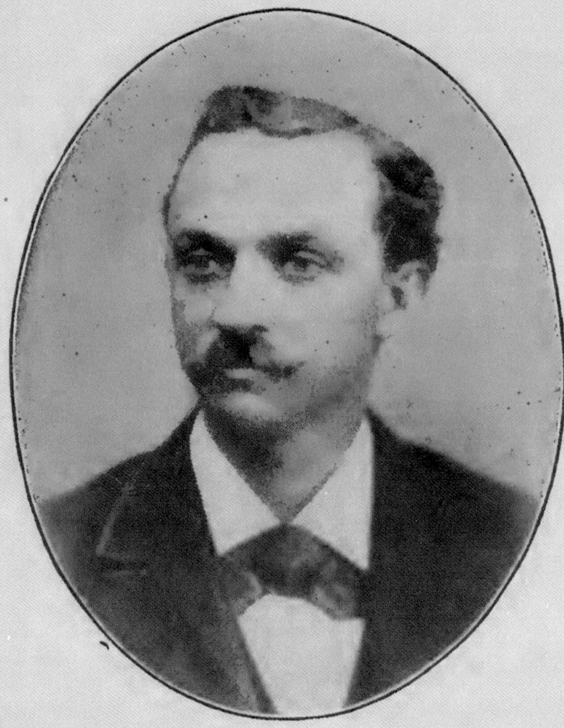

CHARLES TOMLIN

BRADLEY BROTHERS
W. J. BRADLEY, SUCCESSOR
PRINTERS
200 S. TENTH STREET
•
PHILADELPHIA

Index

PAGE

Chapter I—Jersey Land 7
Chapter II—Some Slaves of Cape May County 9
Chapter III—Leaves from History 13
Chapter V—Shingle Mining and the Last Shingle Miner 19
Chapter VI—Hot Sugar. Tobacco 24
Chapter VII—At Cape May Point 27
Chapter VIII—What to Talk About 31
Chapter IX—Trees 32
Chapter X—Ira and John 39
Chapter XI—Noted Sights 41
Chapter XII—The Freeze to Death Year 51
Chapter XIII—Indian Trails 53
Chapter XIV—Cape May Tornadoes 55
Chapter XV—The King's Highway 59
Chapter XVI—The Key 61
Chapter XVII—Plants for Food and Medicine 62
Chapter XVIII—Missionary to the Lenape Indians 63
Chapter XIX—What Kind of a Model Will You Be? 66
Chapter XX—The Great September Gale 68
Chapter XXI—Sweet Sixteen 74
Chapter XXII—Almost Ninety-five 76
Chapter XXIII—Skirmish at Town Bank 79
Chapter XXIV—The Douglass Family 82
Chapter XXV—A Heroine Where I'd Live. Our Albino 90
Chapter XXVI—A Prisoner in Dixie 93
Chapter XXVII—A Romance 111

THIS BOOK

is respectively dedicated to my pupils of the Public Schools in the Counties of Cape May, Cumberland and Atlantic, in the State of New Jersey, whom I have had the honor of trying to instruct, viz.:

1875-6—Swaintown (Erma).
1876—West Creek (Eldora).
1876--7-8 Heislerville.
1878-9-80-81 Ludlam's, Dennisville.
1881-2—Swainton (Erma).
1882-3—Academy, Dennisville.
1883-4—Dias Creek.
1884-5- Academy, Dennisville.
1885-6-7-8-9—Goshen.
1889-90—Green Creek.
1890-1-2-3-4—Academy, Dennisville.
1894-5-6—Port Norris.
1896-7-8-9—Newport.
1899-1900-1-2-3—Dias Creek.
1903-4-5-6-7-8—Woodbine.
1908-9—Dennis Township.
1909-10—Cape May Point.
1910-11—Rio Grande.
1911-12-13—Tuckahoe, Weymouth Township.
1913-14—Dias Creek.

CHAPTER I.

JERSEY LAND.

(*Tune, Dixie Land.*)

So glad I live in the land of peaches
Down nearby the Cape May beaches,
Look away! Look away! Look away! Jersey land:
New Jersey land where I was born,
Early on one frosty morning,
Look away! Look away! Look away! Jersey land:

Chorus:

Then I'm glad I am in Jersey,
  Hoo-ray! Hoo-ray!
In Jersey Land I'll take my stand
To live and die in Jersey,
  Away, away,
Away down in South Jersey,
  Away, away,
Away down in South Jersey,

The land of oysters, clams and mosquitoes,
Potpie, fish and sweet potatoes,
Look away! Look away! Look away! Jersey land:
There's hills of sand and best of bathing,
Sleighing snows with ice and skating,
Look away! Look away! Look away! Jersey land:

Oh, sing of South Jersey's fragrant air,
Of its health and beauty everywhere,
Look away! Look away! Look away! Jersey land:
Of its lassies fair and its lads so bright,
Its schools, farms, factories and electric lights,
Look away! Look away! Look away! Jersey land:

It is washed by the old Atlantic blue
And by the noble Delaware too,
Look away! Look away! Look away! Jersey land:
The sounds are fine for sport and game,
The beach resorts are far from tame,
Look away! Look away! Look away! Jersey land:

The ocean may chill, mosquitoes may bite,
But Delaware Bay is warmed just right,
Look away! Look away! Look away! Jersey land:
For a boy to bathe both day and night,
So shout South Jersey with all your might,
Look away! Look away! Look away! Jersey land:

Sure this is the land of cream and honey,
Everything is grown for money,
Look away! Look away! Look away! Jersey land:
Every mother says to her sonny,
"Grow up great and be somebody,"
Look away! Look away! Look away! Jersey land:

The boys reply "We will do our best
And all good knowledge we will test,"
Look away! Look away! Look away! Jersey land:
The girls reply, "We are up-to-date,"
This age we'll help make good and great,"
Look away! Look away! Look away! Jersey land:

All honor to our sires who chose this spot,
Not frigid cold nor torrid hot;
Look away! Look away! Look away! Jersey land:
As Washington's patriots brave and true,
They in the sixties (1861-5) wore the blue,
Look away! Look away! Look away! Jersey land:

CHAPTER II

SOME SLAVES OF CAPE MAY CO., N. J.

Near the N. W. Corner of the Methodist Episcopal Cemetery, in Goshen, N. J., is a grave marked "Lauring Coatsman, aged 98 years. Faithful Unto Death."

This marks the grave of a colored woman known most of her life by the name of "Vinie". She was a slave and manumitted by John Hand, October 26, 1803, as Vina Armour, being at that time over 21 and under 40 years of age. There is a lady now (1913) living in Philadelphia who remembers hearing her mother tell of a remark made by said lady's father upon a very cold night, "If Bill Coach gets down drunk tonight he will freeze to death" and he did. He was Vinie's husband.

Vinie seems to have been born about 1771 and to have lived till 1869, having lived through the Revolution, the war of 1812, the Mexican and the Civil war days.

Vinie was a very estimable person, loved and respected by many. The tombstones that now mark her grave were placed there by Mrs. Deborah (Wm.) Garrison, a daughter of John and Deborah Hand, whom Vinie had probably served many a day as nurse. Mrs. Garrison, who, 15 years later, died at the age of 86 years, looked after Vinie and made her comfortable in her old age.

Many remember Vinie by her purge beer and cake stand which she kept at many a vendue, ship launching or other big gathering. Her beer was made of herbs,barks etc. selected and gathered by herself, being quite bitter and purgative.

RUMY

Rumy, a slave in Nathaniel Holmes's family, lies buried in the Baptist cemetery at Cape May Court House, N. J., beside

whose tombstone has sprung up a cedar tree so close thereto that it is difficult to read the name. She died Feb. 2, 1858, in her 83rd year.

Many of the colored people of this County who live at Cold Spring, and to the east of Goshen and near Swain Station seem to be descendants of the early slaves of Cape May County.

ELSIE

Elsie who afterward became the wife of Rev. John West, was a slave in Jedediah Tomlin's family and in his will made in 1815 he wills his servant girl Elsie Smith, whom he purchased of Samuel Jones, to his wife Elizabeth, from his death to December 25, 1826, and when set free she was to have two suits of clothes, one common and one Sunday suit.

Elsie is remembered as a devout Christian of a refined and obliging maner. She has descendants living now near Goshen, N. J. She did not remain a slave as late as 1826, because her freedom was purchased by the man whom she married. Her mistress also remarried and became the wife of Cresse Townsend some months before Elsie's term of service as a slave expired.

Aaron Leaming, I, who died in 1747, left slaves. Elisha Hand and Richard Crawford, Appraisers of his property valued them as follows: Tony 15 pounds, No Name 40 pounds Cyrus 35 pounds, Cyrus 28 pounds, Sam 14 pounds, Jonah 7 pounds, Joann 34 pounds, Dido, daughter of Joann 25 pounds, Amy, daughter of Peggy, 15 pounds, Maria 8 pounds.

The original owners of slaves were compelled to care for them in old age.

SLAVES OF CAPE MAY COUNTY, N. J.

SLAVES OF MIDDLE TOWNSHIP.

Ishmael Armour, manumitted by Levi Smith in 1803; Vina Armour, manumitted by John Hand in 1803; Priscilla

Anderson, manumitted by Joseph Mulford in 1808; Ishmael Armour, aged 25, manumitted by John Townsend in 1826; Edward Cox, aged 35, manumitted by Persons Leaming in 1804; Abel Cox, manumitted by Persons Leaming in 1806; Amy Coachman, manumitted by Aaron and Furman Leaming in 1808; Flowra Cox, aged 32, manumitted by Philip Stites in 1802, wife of Abel Cox; James Green, manumitted by Abigail Townsend in 1812; Armindy, manumitted by Nathaniel Holmes in 1808; Harmon Lively, manumitted by Nathaniel Holmes, afterward of Trenton, N. J., in 1815; Marshal Peterson, manumitted by Robert M. Holmes in 1815; Susan Turner, manumitted by Robert M. Holmes in 1819; Betty Jacocks, manumitted by Judith Townsend and Humphrey Swain in 1823; Eace, manumitted by Seth Hand in 1803; Selance, manumitted by Christopher Ludlam in 1803; Scene Turner, manumitted by Persons Leaming in 1807; Derrick Turner, manumitted by Furman Leaming, late of Middle, now of Philadelphia, in 1819; Ruhama Scott, manumitted by Humphrey Stites in 1806; Simeon Taylor, manumitted by Christopher Smith in 1815; Bethula Mingo, manumitted by Elijah Townsend in 1807; Elizabeth Jacock, manumitted by Elijah Townsend in 1811.

SLAVES OF DENNIS TOWNSHIP.

Jethro Alingo, manumitted by Nathaniel Holmes in 1834; Isaac and Amy Jackson were slaves of Henry Ludlam. He had them to get married. They raised several children. There are many people now living who remember their son Augustus Cæsar Jackson.

SLAVES OF UPPER TOWNSHIP.

Marshal Briant, manumitted by Thomas Beesley, in 1832; Benjamin Coachman, Jr., manumitted by Jeremiah Hand, of Upper, in 1806; Francis Coachman, manumitted by Jacob Godfrey, in 1810; Dempcey Collins, manumitted by Jacob

Willets in 1816; Judith Somers, manumitted by Elizabeth Ludlam in 1806; Robert Smith, manumitted by John Van Gilder, Dec. 2, 1809. He had purchased the slave one day before for $100, from James Godfrey of Maurice River Township, Cumberland County, and of Nicholas Godfrey, of Weymouth Township, Gloucester County. Negro Derrick was a slave in the family of Parmenas Corson of Seaville, and was for a long time a regular attendant of Calvary Baptist Church. We think he lies buried in the family plot of his master at Palermo.

SLAVES OF LOWER TOWNSHIP.

James Lively, manumitted by Jesse and Elias Hughes in 1805; Cæsar, manumitted by Thomas H. and Israel Hughes in 1812; Job Moor, manumitted by Thomas H. Hughes in 1828; Peter Murkin, manumitted by Aaron Hughes in 1818; Anthony Wanton manumitted by James R. Hughes in 1817; Nancy Coachman, manumitted by John Stites in 1802; Orris Cox, manumitted by Robert Cox in 1832; Dinah, manumitted by Ann Edmunds in 1808; Susan, manumitted by Joseph Hughes in 1805.

The number of slaves in Cape May County, N. J., were in 1738, 42; 1790, 141; 1800, 98; 1810, 81; 1820, 28; 1830, 3.

There is a deed for a colored burying ground a mile or two north of Cape May Court House, one grave has a marked granite stone on which is cut the name Angelina Taylor. Several persons who had been slaves are said to have been buried there. Among them Aunt Thilda, Cupbalo and wife, Prudie. Aunt Peggy Seagraves, Uncle Alpheus Seagraves, Sr., Alpheus Seagraves, Jr.

CHAPTER III.

LEAVES FROM HISTORY.

Arranged by Charles Tomlin from "Scheyichbi and the Strand," by Edward S. Wheeler.

August 28, 1609, Henry Hudson in the Half Moon sailed into Delaware bay, and not finding the N. W. pasage to India sailed north along the New Jersey coast, anchoring inside of Sandy Hook September 3rd.

Cornelius Jacobson May, who in 1614 commanded the Fortune from Holland and explored from Manhattan to Martha's Vineyard, came again in 1620 in a vessel called the Glad Tidings, and carefully explored Delaware Bay and river, then returning to Holland reported certain new populous and fruitful lands along the Delaware river.

In 1622 May came in the New Netherland to New Netherland as first Director, with thirty families, mostly Walloons. 18 Walloons were left at Manhattan, others at Fort. Orange (now Albany, N. Y.), also five miles below Philadelphia on the Jersey shore Fort Nassau was completed, and four couples of Waloons, who had been married on the New Netherland during her two months' voyage, were sent here in June in a yacht to abide. They remained unharmed during May's directorship and until about 1645 or 7.

The Indians were as quite as lambs, and traded with all freedom imaginable, for May acted in the spirit of the instructions received from his superiors in Holland, who wrote "'Tis better to govern by love and friendship than by force."

Admirers of Captain May have reason to be proud that the southern cape of New Jersey bears the name of May, a study of whose life recalls only deeds of courage and goodness such as confer an honest fame in the history of time and crown with happiness the pure in heart amid the glories of eternity.

As Superintendent of the company of Charter of Freedom and Exemptions, Pieterzen De Fries sent the ship Whale under the command of Pieter Heyes to Delaware bay, founding in 1631 Swandale in the rich territory selected in 1629 for Goodyn and Blommaert. Swandale flourished for a time, but on account of difficulties with the Indians the people were killled and the village burned.

DeVries afterward in 1633 came over as patroon and commander of Swandale and Cape May. He captured wild turkeys weighing as much as 36 pounds. He found fur trading more valuable than the whale fishery. In 1643, on his way to Virginia, he was again in Delaware bay. David Pieterzen DeVries was one of the finest characters of New Netherland history. A man of the people; a foe to despotism, injustice and cruelty. The Indians trusted him as a Swanekin "who never lied like the others." His tact and discrimination more than once saved the province from destruction. Though filling only a subordinate position, DeVries was by nature and experience equally commendable as a man, a citizen and a statesman. It would be untrue to history and unjust to him and his creed not to record in addition the fact that the first resident patroon and owner of Cape May was a man of religious sentiments, in principle, after the best Ideal, a devout and consistent Christian.

September 22, 1909, the people of Delaware held at Lewes a celebration and unveiled a monument of DeVries, on which is inscribed "Erected by the State of Delaware to commemorate the settlement on this spot of the first Dutch colony under DeVries A.D. 1631." Here was the cradling of a state. That Delaware exists as a separate state was due to this colony." State and U. S. officers, U. S. Minister from the Netherlands, as well as war ships from both countries took part in this celebration.

Gillet Hosset and Peter Heyes came from Swandale, Delaware, to the Jersey shore as agents of Goodyn and Blommaert and bought of ten Indian chiefs, on May 5th, 1630, a tract of

land twelve miles along the shore of the bay from Cape May Point to the north, and twelve miles inland above and including Cape May.

The lands on the northern and eastern shores of Delaware bay were in possession of the great and influential but peaceable Indian tribe called Lenni Lennape, from whom must have been obtained the original title to Cape May. As Hosset sailed over the Delaware, he saw a roadstead large enough for all the commerce of Europe to ride secure; dense forests were near the shore, the waters swarmed with fish, the marshes abounding in water-fowl, and game birds, also great and small animals for food and furs. Wm. Penn mentions turkeys weighing from 45 to 50 pounds each.

The Indian resorted to the shore of the Atlantic not alone for health and comfort, but to make money, and to dry the luscious bivalve on white oak splints for their winter store. In Cape May a "mint" was kept in operation, where suskauhock was coined in the form of beads from shells of the quahog and strung on strings. This was sometimes woven into belts. This is why the great beds of shells found hereabouts are in such small pieces. They were broken to secure the dark part of the shell, as this formed the most valuable money, though there was good white wampum made of the stem of the periwinkle, yet only one-half as valuable as the suskauhock.

All honor to Wm. Penn for the great work he did after 1682 for the great state that bears his name, but let it be remembered that in West Jersey his inspired mind and benevolent heart FIRST wrought out his model of a state between 1675 and 1680, and there alone his purpose first became the law and rule of a happy people. Every acre of New Jersey has been fairly bought of the Indian tribes. West Jersey is unstained by Indian blood. Indians, Puritans, Quakers, and Covenanters, held in peace and universal prosperity the soil of New Jersey.

John Worlidge and John Budd, coming down from Burlington, laid off a tract of land in Cape May county for Dr.

Coxe in 1687, on which he built Coxe Hall as a residence. Cape May was cut off from the north by vast impassable cedar swamps that extended from the seashore to the bay. Cape May was set off as a county in 1692.

America won in the war of 1812-14, because of finer modeled, better rigged, and more "handy" vessels; and because on those vessels, for the first time, long range guns and cannon were supplied with "sights," and trained with the deadly accuracy of the rifle on the mark. It was precision against mass or as a thunderbolt to a hail storm. Many Cape May men were very active in this war.

In closing, we again pay homage to the noble lives, deeds and influence of May, DeVries and Penn on and for West Jersey.

/

CHAPTER IV.

PIRATES.

Captain Kidd and also Blackbird visited New Jersey. Once when the latter was off our coast and landed east of Burleigh one Uncle Aaron and his wife aunt Becky were on a cowshed intently watching his operations as they killed cattle and loaded them into small boats taking them aboard the ship to dress and clean. Aunt Becky kept stepping around when all of a sudden a cannon was fired which caused her to step a little more lustily and farther backward, when all of a sudden she tumbled off backward in a heap a distance of twelve or fifteen feet. This fall almost unjointed her neck, and being otherwise injured it was a long time before she fully recovered remembering to the end of her days Blackbeard's visit near her home.

BLOCK HOUSE

The last old block house in the county with its port holes, palisades and made of the choicest white cedar logs, seems to have stood at Mosquito Point, in N. W. Dennis. The logs were taken for a time and used as a corn crib but finally converted into lumber.

Two Ludlam brothers settled, one on the north and the other on the south side of Dennis Creek, and this block house stood near the road now leading to Jake's Landing, where most likely was first the fording place, then a ferry, then farther east was built the old stage road, the remains of which remain today on the meadow of John Williams. In later years came the present route over the once covered bridge.

OLD FORT.

In South Dennis at the junction of Sluice and Dennis creeks is the foundation of an old fort said to antedate the

days of the Revolutionary war. Said fort was placed and maintained there to protect the settlers hereabouts from the depredations of pirates and privateers. Great were the hardships and privations of our forefathers and greater yet their perseverance, determination and ability. Savages, pirates, a wild country, many things of which we little dream did they encounter and yet they endured and conquered.

CHAPTER V.

SHINGLE MINING AND THE LAST OF OUR SHINGLE MINERS.

Out of the lowlands near Dennisville, N. J., millions of dug up shingles have been mined.

To the best of my knowledge the last miner, an intelligent, clear minded gentlemen and a lover of history, was Charles Pitman Robart who died in 1907, in his 79th year.

One of his greatest finds consisted of a log four feet in diameter and 25 feet in length. On top of this was another log fully as large and above both was a partially decayed stump from which had been taken a tree of about the same diameter. Growing in the decayed part of this stump was a live tree fully a foot in diameter in a good healthy condition. The under log must have lain there for centuries.

This tree was much better than the ordinary from the fact it was so fine a rift and perfectly sound throughout and so far up it before any limbs were found. The shingles therefrom sold for $75. Trees as large as this were frequently found but they would often turn out to be knotty or hard.

These miners took an iron rod six to eight feet long sharpened at one end and by pushing it down in meadow or swamp lands would progue until they struck a log. Then beginning near the top end would saw off under the mud a piece of the log about a foot in length, called the "cut-off," which in water would turn over pop up and float like cork. They, by its smell, could tell if it was a wind fall or a broke down.

The piece would also tell them if the tree was boxy, twisted or straight grained. If it proved to be desirable then with a cross cut saw, having a long handle, the tree was sawn free of its limbs and roots along its whole length upon two sides. This freed it of most limbs and roots that held it fast.

The butt end was then sawed loose and pried to the surface. Blocks, pries etc. were then used until the whole log was brought nearly to or upon the surface. It was then sawed into proper lengths for shingles. These blocks were then split into smaller blocks called dolts. A dolt would make four shingles. These rough shingles after being split from the dolts were dried in the sun, then shaved with a drawing knife and made straight on the edge with a jointer so as to lay close edge to edge. They were also usually butted, that is, the butt cut off across its entire width at an angle of about 45 degrees with a tool of triangular shape having three legs with cross pieces near their center to which was fastened a long knife, its outer end had a handle by which it was worked up and down while its lower end was stationary turning only around a bolt. This butting machine was about three feet in height. Many of these shingles were six inches wide and usually eighteen inches long and one-half inch thick at the but end tapering gradually to a point at the other end.

It was not customary to mine logs that were more than six feet below the surface of the ground.

A quarter share went to the owner of the land when the mining was in live timber, but a one-eighth share elsewhere.

We can best continue this sketch by quoting from a letter from Mr. Edwin Robart, son of Mr. Charles P. Robart. He says "father was the son of Samuel Robart and of German descent. Father's great- grandfather lived in the days of the Revolution near Great Egg Harbor Inlet, and was one of sixteen to man a large boat that was propelled with oars, having on its bow a small cannon. When ever they saw a merchantman becalmed off the Inlet, this crew would man their boat and investigate. If it proved to be an English vessel, she would be taken as a prize and brought into the Inlet.

Once this crew sighted what looked like an English merchantman becalmed, so taking their boat they rowed toward the same. When they were near enough they discharged their cannon and hailed the ship to surrender, when lo! the ship

dropped her ports and run out four guns. It was an English sloop-of-war, and such rowing as those men did soon brought them out of range.

My experience with my father in removing these logs from the soil and converting them into shingles was, from the time I arrived at the age of ten until I was sixteen years of age, always in the summer when out of school.

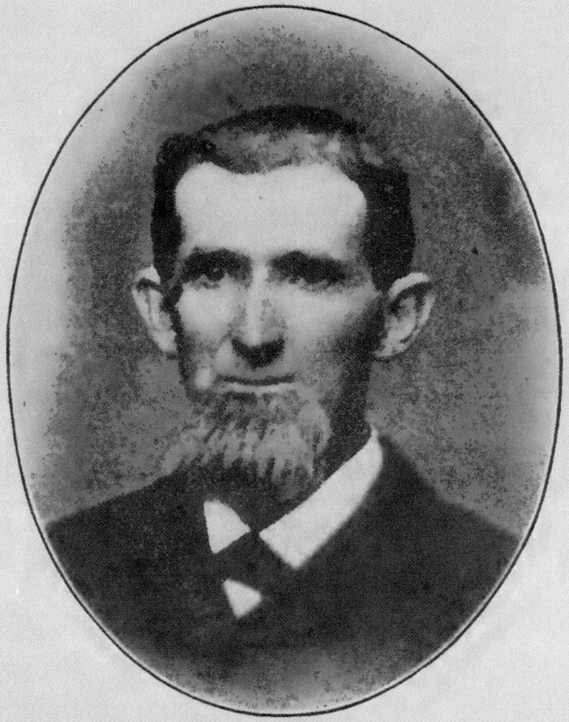

C. P. ROBART

Shingles were secured in Brick Landing swamp, South Dennis, head of Dennis Creek, back and on the meadows below what is known as Mosquito Point. On the bald meadows where there was no sign of any swamp below on banks of what is called the Folly, a stream, one and a half miles long, flowing from the north into Dennis Creek, about three miles below Jake's landing.

No doubt the greatest place where these logs were found was in what is known as Robbin's swamp. This swamp was cut off about 1864, enabling miners to investigate the bottom. The result was that hundreds of thousands of these shingles were taken out as there were several shingle miners at that time. Roads had been made from poles and bark to get the live timber out, and these same roads were used to cart out these shingles. Shingles secured in most places had to be carried out on the backs of men and boys to the creek and then taken by boat to the landing.

Besides supplying the local market, these shingles were sent by regular packet boats to be sold in Philadelphia or towns on the Delaware River. Sometimes they would be taken to some place in the state of Delaware and there traded for corn and the corn brought to Dennis Creek landing and then sold to some dealer in grain before any money could be realized by the miner. Father secured thousands of these shingles in what is known as Hawk swamp. Here is where my mind is fully clear, as here so many had to be carried on our backs to the roads. I being a boy could carry but twelve of these shingles if they were shaven as soon as they were dug, which was quite frequently the case. If the shingles could be dug and allowed to dry thoroughly a man could make much more headway in shaving them. Father was considered a fast workman and could shave six hundred a day. With things favorable he could mine and get ready for market one thousand shingles per week which usually sold for $16.00. In later years when the sawed shingles came on the market, the price was as low as $12.00, which was very poor pay for mined shingles. The present roof on Independence Hall, Philadelphia, is of dug up shingles secured in Cape May Co. Mr. John Anneley secured the contract for 25,000 shingles, and he and father prepared all these shingles and was paid an extra price for the same. Mrs. Sophia Taylor's house in Dennisville is now roofed with dug up shingles that have been on more than eighty years.

Father sent many shingles to Cape May city. I remem-

ber at one time he engaged three teams, he going with them and walking all the way. It was the custom on trips of this character to start as soon as the load was on, continue all through the night, stopping only long enough to feed the horses, arriving at Cape May city sometime the following day. Some of the finest grained wood brought an extra price, being shipped in boxes to dealers in some of the western states to be used in the manufacture of violins. Violins made from this wood gave forth a better quality of music than those made from any other wood.

Tools used in this business were cross-cut saw, progue, drawing knife, butters, maul, ax, drag, and froe. The froe was used in splitting the cuts and also in splitting the shingles after they had been bolted up. The froe is a piece of iron fifteen inches long, three inches wide and one half inch thick on the back or top side tappering to an edge at the bottom having an eye in one end so as to let a handle stick up one foot. A maul about as heavy as a man can lift, is used to strike the froe to make it do the splitting. The but ends of a wind-fall, one that blew down and up at the roots, furnished the best wood but sometimes a break-off would furnish three or four good cuts. For a number of years after the Civil War in which he served, father was engaged in the milling of grain, but after the mill blew out he returned to shingle mining following it until he was 76 years of age.

I have a dug up shingle which is much weathered, 32x8-1-2 inches by one-half inch thick (when new it was one inch thick) taken from the home of Linneus T. Swain, where it has been a side, not roof shingle, since 1785 or earlier, as this house has been known to have been in the family at least that long. In later years these shingles were made shorter and narrower.

The front or westward side of the roof on the front of Mr. Coleman F. Leaming's brick house, late home of the Hon. Richard S. Leaming, is of these dug-up or mined shingles, placed there by his grandfather, Joseph Falkenburge, about 1803 and are giving good service yet (1913) Those on the eastern or back part were removed about 1875.

CHAPTER VI.

HOT SUGAR.

(*Tune—Yankee Doodle*)

Shut in my home by winter's storm
  Snow whirling wild without
A curley-headed little boy
  Runs chattering about.
He seizes now the pepper box,
  Then rushes for his cot,
Back comes a yelling cry of rage,
  "Dis sudar bowl is hot."

Chorus

Keep your eyes on the little tot,
  Also on the bigger lot,
For when the pepper box is not
  Sugar is most likely to be hot.

Oft methought in the race of life
  The sugar-bowl is hot,
For when I tried my first segar
  My supper it was not.
And when the girl I loved so well
  Another fellow got,
Or when my business went to wreck
  They sold my bed and cot.

Then when I sailed old ocean blue
  And sang "New York" or what?
Thinking to never see home again,
  The sugar bowl was hot.
Like t'other end of a little stick

Mother or teacher shook,
Or best end of a business deal
The other fellow took.

Once 'long came a confidence man,
Another with folding cot,
When home burned down—a total loss—
The sugar bowl was hot.
At a show, a horse race too,
I saw my last cent trot,
Whenever I take the crooked road
The sugar bowl gets hot.

In order to make a living
Or keep what you have got,
Eye well the other fellow or
He'll make your sugar hot.
So now my boy, my little girl,
Fill up your brain with meat,
So when you're old and have to strive
Your sugar will not heat.

Don't waste your time by hanging round
With a low, filthy lot,
Should ever it come your time to crow
You'll find your sugar hot.
Don't fool around a drinking place
'Twill cause your brain to rot,
So gambling and those games of chance
May make your sugar hot.

Then seek the right, my little one,
The good, the great, the true,
If nobly you seek wisdom's ways
Life will be sweet to you.

You'll crow, and sing, and shout, and jump,
  And rest and love and eat,
Because you've loved to help the weak
  Your sugar's cool and sweet.

TOBACCO.

Tobacco is an excellent pill
For lice and insects pests to kill,
Good to dull the brain and weaken the heart
And make one any thing else than smart.
Said to be a filthy weed
And from the devil to proceed,
Robbing the pockets, burning one's clothes
Making a chimney of one's nose,
Stinking its user from head to toes
So whether to use tobacco
Or whether to use it not,
The only answer I care to give is
YOU'D BETTER, BETTER NOT.

CHAPTER VII

AT CAPE MAY POINT

From near the eastern end of Lake Lily at Cape May Point is the remains of an old ditch running to the north between the farms of Alvin B. Marcy and John Reeves for more than three-quarters of a mile into Pond Creek.

At one place where the timber has lately been converted into logs and cordwood, the ditch is now (1910) from two to 16 feet deep, going through sand banks as well as meadow land.

Tradition says this ditch was dug to let salt water into Lake Lily to prevent the British from getting supplies of fresh water therefrom. Note well the grit, determination, patience and perseverance of our patriot ancestors. Once when ashore here stealing cattle and getting water, one of the British asked a patriot what kind of buildings were two houses nearby that had Dormer windows? Oh, replied the American, who like so many others in this country, ready at all times to outwit the British even when they could not whip them, "they are houses used for army quarters and those windows in the roof are port holes, and in a few minutes you'll be mown down with shot from the guns which the soldiers there have nearly ready to fire." Such hustling of the casks of water and the hurrying of the cattle and sheep to the small boats and then to the ship was laughable to behold.

Edward S. Wheeler records that once The Pontiers, a British line-of-battle ship in 1812 appeared off Cape May city and threatened to bombard the place if its inhabitants did not supply them with fresh water. The cheap ransom was paid at once and the ship sailed away. Probably this happened soon after they had been deprived of getting fresh water from Lake Lily by the letting in thereto of salt water.

Cape May Point, a place of natural beauty; the ocean meeting the bay, the rips, the setting sun, the cedars bending low from strong winds, their limbs trailing close to or upon the ground, the incoming and outgowing ships of all kinds and sizes, and that beautiful lake (Lake Lily) for boating, skating, rowing, ice-boating, with Amnon island for a landing place within its waters, the bridge across its eastern end with the mass of lilies and other flowers, contrasting with the adjoining sand dunes some wooded and others not. Cottages in groves, some not in groves, and down upon all each night shines the great Cape May light revolving, lighting the darkness, warning the sailor as well as acting as his guide, and beautifying Cape May Point and its surrounding waters.

THE CAPE MAY LIGHTHOUSE.

The English government built the Cape Henlopen lighthouse on the western or opposite shore of Delaware Bay in 1744, and it is very probable that the first Cape May lighthouse was built by them on its eastern shore where the ocean meets the bay at about the same date. Old ocean has rolled for years where the first lighthouse stood. A second which was built in 1823 is now about 500 feet from high water mark and is used as a stable.

The third and present one built in 1859, stands about 1000 feet from high water mark. It is 100 feet in circumference at its base and 180 feet in height, and has within it a spiral stairway of 199 steps plus eight additional ones above the light. This stairway divided into six flights has at the head of five of This stairway divided into six flights has at the head of each of five of them a resting place and a window. At the head of the sixth is an outside walkway 40 feet around, the revolving light which is alternately bright and dark for 30 seconds each, and the revolving clockwork machinery with its reflector of 550 prisms and 16 lenses. The center of each lense is the center of greatest brilliancy while between each lense and its corres-

ponding prisms is the frame which holds them and furnishes the center for darkness.

The old kerosene lamp which had five concentric wicks and consumed seven and one-half gallons of oil between sunset and sunrise, was replaced about 1910 with a vapor light and as our dear Uncle Sam loves to keep everything of his up-to-date, new clock work machinery took the place of that which had been in constant use for over fifty years.

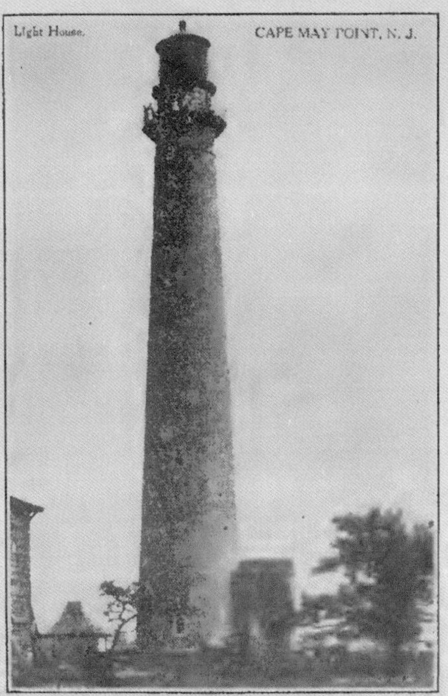

Cape May Light House

The latest information of authority comes to me from the office of Inspector of Fourth District, Philadelphia, Pa., by letter of March 20, 1913. It says:

A Description of Cape May Lighthouse Tower.

The tower is constructed of brick laid in cement mortar. The walls at the base are about eight feet thick; at the top 24

inches thick. The diameter of the lighthouse at the base is 27 feet; at the top 15 feet. From the base of the structure to the top of the lantern is 170 feet.

This consists of a revolving lens manufactured by Henry Lepaute, Paris, France. The lens is of the first order and has an inside diameter of six feet. The whole lens revolves on ball-bearing chariots. Time of one revolution eight minutes. The light gives a flash every 30 seconds, which can be seen for 19 miles. The lens is revolved by means of a weight actuated clock. The light is produced by incandescent oil vapor and has a candle power of 210,000. This Light Station is in charge of three keepers, one of whom is always on watch at nights. This light is used as a coast light.

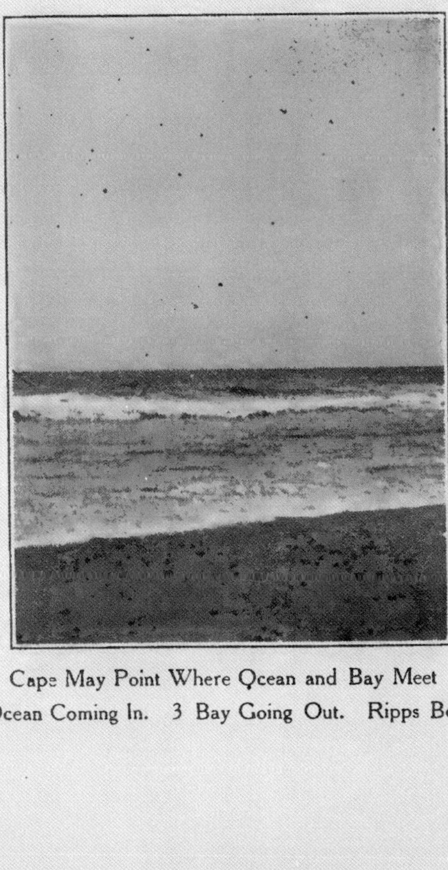

Cape May Point Where Ocean and Bay Meet

1 Strand. 2 Ocean Coming In. 3 Bay Going Out. Ripps Between. 5 Sky

CHAPTER VIII.

WHAT TO TALK ABOUT.

When a friend comes around
  For a chat or a visit,
Talk of naught that is low,
  Speak of the grand the exquisite.

Tell what makes the body healthy,
  Tell what makes the mind grow,
Say what causes the soul's graces
  To quicken and overflow.

Talk of what is pleasing,
  Speak of that which is grand,
Of deeds that ennoble
  Throughout this great land.

Read of heroic deeds,
  Of the many new delights,
Read of the new inventions
  And the many pleasing sights.

Speak of pleasant times, Study
  Industries that are new,
Say what makes man better,
  Say what makes man true.

Talk of noble manhood,
  Speak of their saintly wives,
Speak of pleasant landscapes,
  And bright and sunny skies.

You'll be growing grander,
  Then you'll be growing wise,
Making yourself and others
  Happy this side the skies.

CHAPTER IX.

LOMBARDY POPLARS.

Often called "Sky Poplars" because of their great height. On the homestead of the late John Goff who for many years was the village blacksmith of West Creek (Eldora), Cape May Co., is probably the tallest sky poplar to be seen at this time (1913) in this county.

Tradition says that they were planted as a protection from lightning. Being so much taller than the dwelling houses lightning would naturally take to them instead of to the house.

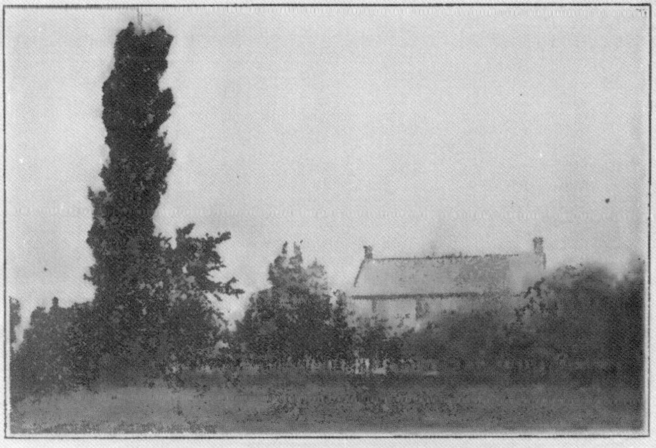

Lombardy Poplars often called "Sky Poplars"

History says our patriot forefathers planted them in Colonial days to denote the growth of liberty in this country believing that as these trees grew in height the spirit of liberty grew more and greater in the hearts of the American people. Facts seem to prove that their belief was well founded.

These trees bear no fruit and give so little shade that some have been surprised to see the remains of them in so many places, but each one marks the home plot of a plantation

where lived a patriot and not a tory. Think how many times these old plantations have been divided and redivided among heirs since the Revolution and the surprise is that the farms of today are as large as they are yet it serves to show the immense size of those old plantations.

A pleasant sight of my boyhood days—the days of the Civil War—was to see "Old Glory" fly from the top of a pole that protruded 25 feet out of the top of one of these 50 feet high "sky poplars" on the farm of the late "Uncle Billy Douglass" then an old man, and he it was who induced the frightened inhabitants of the Delaware Bay shore to place Quaker guns (gum logs shaped and painted like cannon) along the Delaware Bay shore from the Cedar Hammocks southward during the war of 1812, when the British ships sailed into the bay.

CEDAR.

Then there is a very old cedar tree with a strong eastern inclination on the eastern side of the bay shore road and near

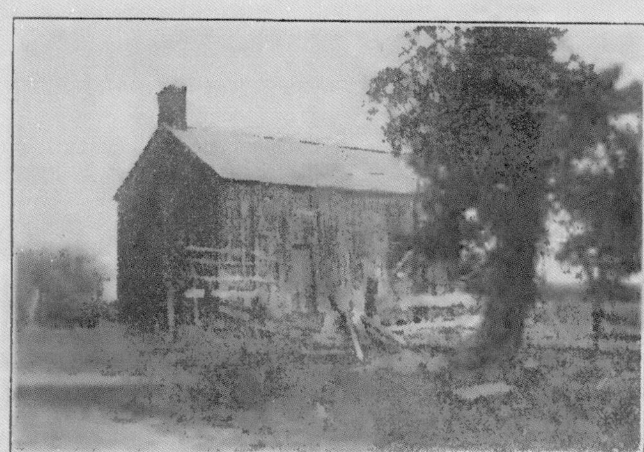

Cedar and Old Preaching Place

to the first road south of Dennisville, as well as Goshen that branches off to drive to the shore of old Delaware Bay where adjoining this said road on its north lay father's farm where

we have helped gather hundred of tons of salt and sedge hay and many tons of gravel to ship to Philadelphia for roofing houses. Here close to the "Cedar Hammocks" we have been poisoned by its ivy and have caught thousands of king crabs as they came to lay their eggs in the warm strand of this shore and then helped to convert them into many tons of cancerine—the greatest fertilizer extant.

But returning to our cedar we wish to say that it stands near an old house that was formerly the old preaching place below Goshen where many a strong sermon and good class as well as prayer meeting has been held. This old house is now owned by Mr. Elisha B. Scull, beneath and around this cedar gathered our forefathers and many generations since have played beneath this partially-bared-trunk cedar tree.

THE TWO LINDENS.

Two beautiful linden trees stand near Johnson Lake in Cape May County soil at Dennisville, N. J., in front of the home of Miss Rhoda Beesley. These trees were in 1811 a present to Miss Sarah L. Moore, who afterward became the wife of the late Dr. Maurice Beesley, who for a number of

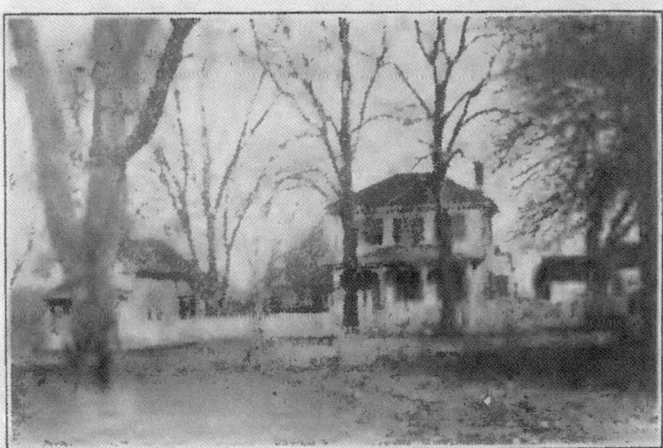

The Two Lindens

years was superintendent of the public schools of this county.

An only brother, Leaming Moore, son of Amos C. Moore and Hannah his wife, presented them to his sister when she was but five years old, and so choice were they that he paid $5.00 each to get them.

Amos C. Moore was a major in the war of 1812, and as he did not die until 1857 and as these trees stand on the soil that was formerly his home they have already given their refreshing shade to three, yea four generations of his family and bid fair to give shade for many years to come. The bark of the bass or linden tree is in some places used to make cordage and mats.

THE TWO MULBERRIES.

There are several white mulberry trees in this county. Called white because their fruit is white in color and to distinguish them from the mulberry that bears fruit of a darkish

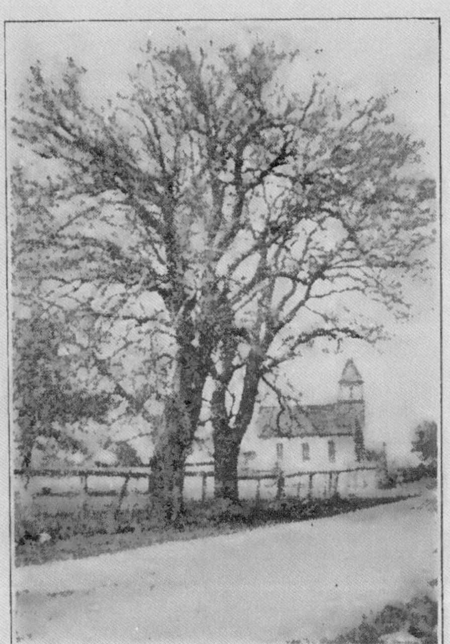

The Two Mulberries

red. Most likely the largest and oldest are the two standing on the farm of Charles Tomlin at Dias Creek, N. J., a few rods south of the Baptist Church. They were set out to furnish food for the silk worm when the silk-raising industry was being tried hereabouts. So many years ago that we fail to find out when these trees were set. They are from three to four feet in diameter with a circumference of ten and one-half and twelve feet, and doubtless are over one hundred years old.

The industry proved to be not a financial success, for what reason I know not. Whether the climate, the want of knowing how to manage the business or what I've been unable to learn, though word comes to me that any new or questionable scheme was thereafter spoken of as "Probably another Mulla Caulus," yet New Jersey today ranks as the first state in the production of silk, even if in early days it failed in Cape May county.

THE BIG POPLAR.

On Brower Island near the head of the Beaver Dam swamp in the vicinity of the Tommy Townsend mill property (now owned by Mr. Frank Leaming) lay in 1876 a fallen poplar tree of such immense proportions that the Hon. Richard S. Leaming was asked to send a portion of it to the Centennial Exhibition. The task was one too big to be granted. This tree measured about nine feet in diameter and fifty feet to its first limb. Fires have destroyed it. Only an outline of its immense stump can be seen. About 1865 a gang of thieves prowled about various parts of this county robbing cellars, henhouses, cribs, meat houses and such like. On one of these raids a dog was left and held as a decoy. Soon after on one bright moonlight night at Dias Creek, while a young man was courting the girl whom he afterward married, their attention was called to something going on outside. Unarmed he sallied out called to the two men outside and followed them until one reached for a weapon. So bright was the moon that this young man's evidence coupled with the fact that the strange dog had not been gotten out of the corn crib by these two

raiders but was on the same premises the next morning and which was claimed by a certain man a few days afterward that the leader and several members of the gang were landed in jail out of which they broke. Recapture for a long time proved futile. They appeared to be in the county but just where no one seemed to be able to find out. It has been learned since that the hollow of this tree served them as a home and a safe, unsuspected place of concealment.

AN AMERICAN ELM.

About two miles north of the county jail of Cape May County, N. J., on the farm lately purchased by William S.

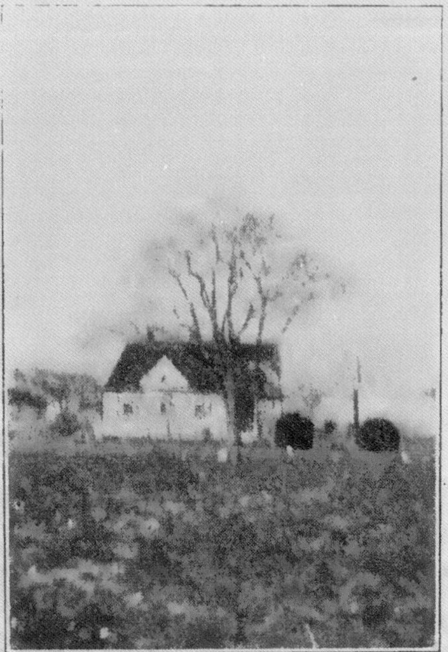

An Ame.ican Elm

Thomas off Mr. Frank Leaming, stands what we believe to be a Boston or American elm, probably fifty feet high and four feet above the ground, has a circumference we judge of fourteen feet. At another place in New Jersey have we heard of

a similar tree, and we believe that they are scions from the Cambridge elm under whose wide spreading branches Washington took command of the American army in 1775.

Jeremiah Ludlam, the grandfather of Frank Leaming, remarked in his latter days that this tree seemed as large 75 years ago as it did then. He died about 1860, and this place was once his homested. Our patriot fathers loved to perpetuate such memories as Washington at Cambridge, and who knows but what some sons of Cape May were in that gathering and that then or afterward they or some relative when visiting Boston procured a scion of said elm and planted it in the soil of old Middle Township, or was it carried by emigrations first to Long Island and then here.

CHAPTER X.

IRA AND JOHN

A group of noble looking American boys stood upon the banks of a stream and decided to swim across it. One whom we shall call Ira, with a physique and bearing more pronounced if possible than the rest, succeeded in reaching its opposite bank first. When finally all had come safely over they praised Ira for being the first to arrive across. Whereupon Ira exclaimed: "That's nothing, I could have done it with a stone tied to one of my feet." His companions doubted it and procured the stone and tied it on and secured a boat and rowed after him to furnish help if he needed any, but Ira crossed safely. Then they praised him more than ever.

A week later about the same group of boys were by the same stream, and in speaking of Ira's former feat, he exclaimed: "I could swim across with a stone tied to each foot!" And so he did.

At another time he boasted that he could do so with a stone tied to a wrist as well as to each foot. This was kept up until he swam the stream with a weight fastened weight fastened to each ankle and wrist and a weight upon his back. He had swam the stream so often and so much weighted that upon this day the boys did not accompany him with a boat, and when about midstream where the tide was unusually strong and the waves were lashed by a strong wind, Ira sank beneath the waters. He had taken one risk—one weight too many.

The summer was drawing rapidly to a close, when one day Ira, a picture of health, tried to swim the stream with a pound weight fastened to each ankle and wrist and a two pound weight upon his back. He had swam the stream so often and so much weighted that upon this day the boys did not accompany him with a boat, and when about midstream

where the tide was unusually strong and the waves were lashed by a strong wind, Ira sank beneath the waters He had taken one risk—one weight too many.

This group of boys is characteristic of every man, woman and child passing through this life. Pure in childhood but many gradually tack on one vice after another until they sink into hell fire.

About the first thing a child begins to branch off from an upright life is disobedience to parents, wanting his own way. So onward down the crooked road, and instead of its being a stone tied to a limb, it is disobedience, lying, smoking, swearing tied to his character. Breaking the first commandment of God, then another and another until very few, if any, are kept. Acting the Ira.

Having other gods or things first in his affections.

Serving or seeking pleasures, riches, honor, fame, where they are not.

Swearing, breaking the Sabbath, lying or bearing false witness and thinking he can carry these and other similar things through life and be a model, upright, prosperous citizen. I tell ye, nay, for in an unguarded moment too many go so far they cannot retrace and they tumble in a heap of disgrace or sink engulfed in sin.

What a contrast to one, however humble his sphere in life may be, who tries to be true to parents and God? Aims to lead a clean life, strives to improve in body, mind and soul, each generation heeding the warnings and avoiding the mistakes of its forefathers, improving given opportunities until upright living and intelligence produce a person or family of brains, power, integrity and manliness, a giant for his or their age and race, honored by God and man as was McKinley, Gladstone and Queen Victoria, and the family of Fields respected on earth and welcomed to heaven. The John's of the ages.

CHAPTER XI.

NOTED SIGHTS.

At Rio Grande, a village about seven miles north of Cape May city, through which passes two main and two branch railroads, the New State Boulevard, and from which runs a fine driveway to Holly Beach, may be seen the remains of the old sorghum sugar mill. Then about a half mile to the north-west on the farm of John Cresse, where an overhead irrigating

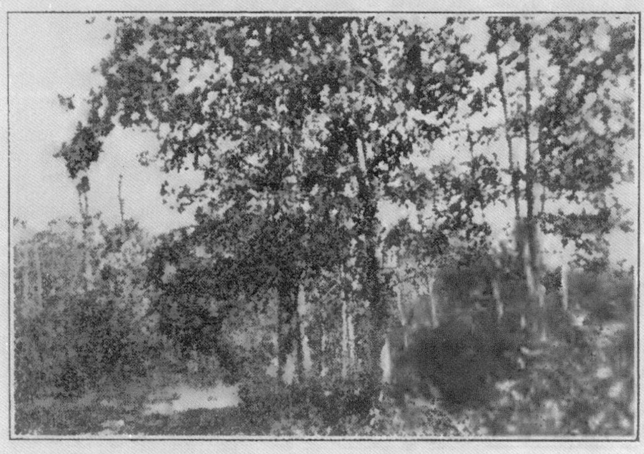

Grove of Nummy Burrying Ground

plant has lately been installed, may be seen a grove, mostly of hickory, in which and in the adjoining fields lie buried in this old Nummy burying ground, hundreds of Indians. Probably as many as 300 natural stones that likely had been brought from Pennsylvania marked these resting places fifty years ago but now very few remain. These stones have been appropriated to various purposes. One man took quite a number to use as ballast for his boat. The chief Indian of these parts was Nummy. His grave is in this grove. A portion of this locality is to this day known as Nummytown, though some of it has of late acquired the name of Green Splinter. Henry

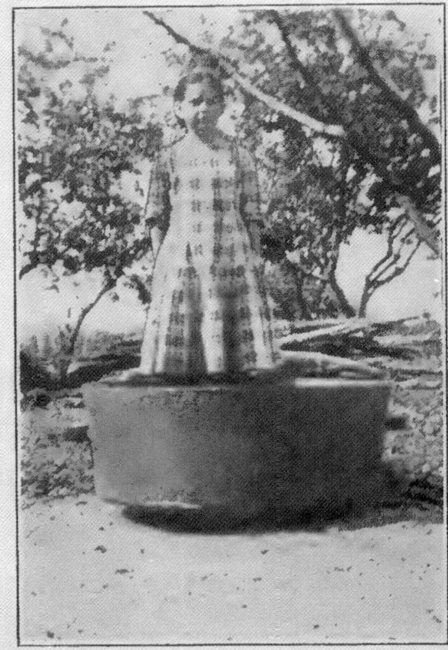

A. C. Hildreth's Boiler
First for Salt, Second, Molasses

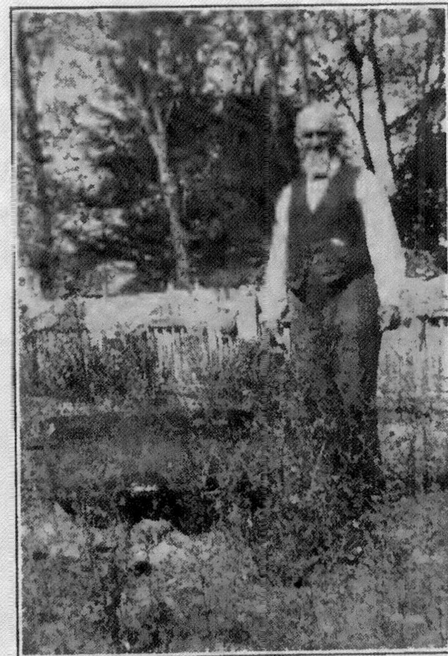

Ephraim Hildreth, III, and the Boiler

Davis formerly owned this farm. History speaks of one Nummy selling a whale to one Evan Davis who owned a plantation about 1685. Perhaps this present farm is a part of that plantation and that it had come down to Henry Davis from this ancestor Evan. History also says that Nummy was the last king or chief of the Lenni Lenapes, and that after he was buried on Nummy Island near Hereford Inlet these Indians left for Indiana and settled on the banks of the Wabash river and never returned to Cape May. This place is so surrounded by swamps, ponds and creeks that the Indians likely considered it an island, and if this message was carried back here from Indiana it is easy to see that to Indians living in Indiana it would be near Hereford. The writer does not believe that Nummy was buried on the Nummy island that is near Hereford inlet close to the Atlantic ocean. Do not think the Indians would bury in a mud island. I am later informed that Nummy island was once covered with large hard yellow pine and this island was the Indians summer home, but Nummytown their winter quarters. Papers found of late prove that Nummy island by Hereford Inlet was left by Parsons Leaming to his daughter Mary, later Mrs. Robert M. Holmes.

On the eastern side of this village at the home of Ephraim Hildreth III, may be seen a large boiler about four feet across and eighteen inches deep in which our forefathers in 1812 boiled salt water producing salt for home uses. Later when quantities of sugar cane was raised hereabouts said boiler was used for boiling its juice to produce molasses. This was years before the sorghum plantation and factory was thought of. Near by on the farm of County Clerk A. Carlton Hildreth, is another boiler of the same kind having been used for the same purposes. Here, too, may be seen some parts of the old cane crushing mill and on an elevation in the meadow near the sound is A. Carlton Hildreth's club house, which is built on the spot where salt was manufactured and is known as Salt Works hill.

Then on the farm lately purchased by Jos. P. McKissic and

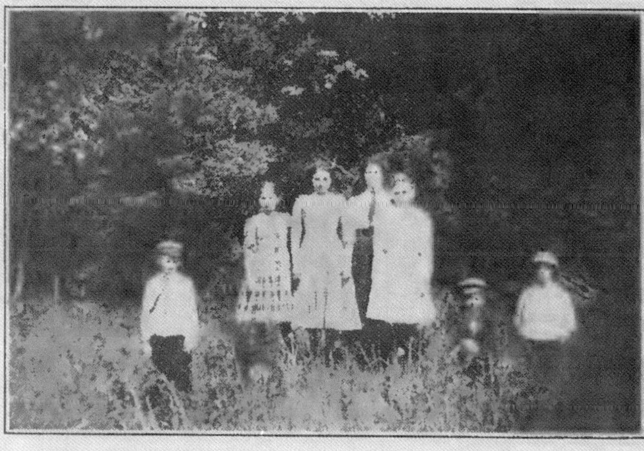

Embankment—Girls on Bank and Boys at its sides

known as the "Richardson" farm and lying between these two Hildreth's farms down near the meadows in its farthest eastern field, is the remains of an old embankment—some say thrown up during the Revolutionary war—others say during the war of 1812, used as a means of defense against the British. One end of said bank has been plowed and leveled but the north end is now (1913) about four feet wide and from two to three feet high. The bank runs in the direction of the remains of an old fort's foundation on the land of Ephraim Hildreth. Likely used as a protection against pirates, privateers and British. Not far from here is Snake creek rising to the south and making near the mainland a short abrupt turn eastward to the ocean. This is the creek the British are said to have come up in their small boats on their raids and here if anywhere occurred a skirmish where the Americans resisted attempts to steal their cattle. For many years and until only a few years ago stood a flourishing flour and grain mill at this Snake creek bend. Since the above was prepared the following article, written by Samuel Springer, who died in 1877 and was a drummer boy in the war of 1812, also sheriff of Cape May County about 1840, was handed to me July 9, 1913.

NUMMIE TOWN AND NUMMIE'S ISLAND.

About seven miles above Cape Island is a place called Nummie Town, situated on the head of Fishing creek midway between Delaware bay and the Atlantic ocean. It takes its name from once being the residence of an Indian chief named Nummie. At this place he had his principal headquarters. King Nummie appears to have understood that the seashore and sea bathing were conducive to health as well as pleasure, and there is no doubt but that he often visited Cape Island to enjoy these luxuries. But his principal place of resort appears to have been an island on the seashore opposite Hereford Inlet. This island named in honor of this Indian chief, was once, no doubt, quite a large place. Those who remember it about the time of the Revolution say there were many acres

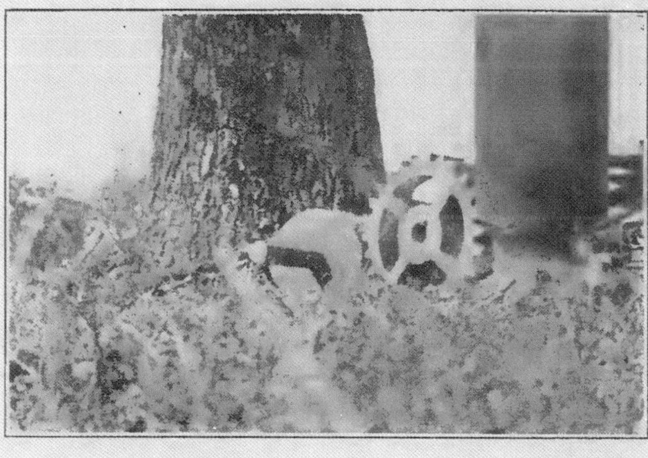

Remains of Old Cane Mill

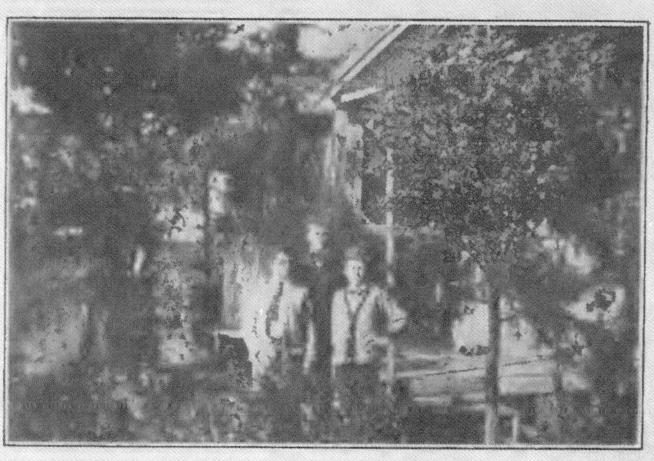

Club House on Salt Works Hill

covered with a heavy growth of red cedar and what is generally called the Indian pine. At that time and indeed long since, it had a fine beach and as it was open to the sea it must have been a delightful summer retreat. King Nummie lived at the time of the settlement of lower Jersey by the Europeans and made this island his principal resort for enjoying the luxuries of the seashore and that he fared sumptously was plain to be seen from the large piles of oyster and clam shells left upon the island.

It was also famous for birds, terripins, etc., and in May and June the whole island was almost litterally covered with birds eggs. There are those now living who have collected a barrel full in a single day. In 1820 a man could collect half a bushel of terripin eggs, and if a laying day, could pick up as many terripins as he could carry. So you see King Nummie must have enjoyed all the luxuries of life, by only reaching out his hand and gathering what came to his tent door. King Nummie was no doubt a friendly Indian, as we have no account of any of those barbarous acts being committed by him which were so common among the Indian at the time of the settlement of the country by the whites. In the year 1692 there were Indians in this county as appears from the records of the first courts. In the second suit on record George Taylor accuseth John Jarvis for helping the Indians to rum. Said Jarvis refusing to clear himself was convicted.

But 165 years have made sad havoc with King Nummie's Island. The high land like all the beaches on the sea coast, was composed of fine sand and Hereford Inlet having broken out directly in front of it laid it open to the surges of the Atlantic, and it has yielded to its constant washing until there is nothing left of that once beautiful island save a few scrub bushes and that part of it composed of meadow which is famous for birds eggs to this day. I have collected all the timber in the neighborhood which came from Nummie's Island which I intend working into canes and presenting to the fair to be held at the island to aid the Baptist Church in that place in

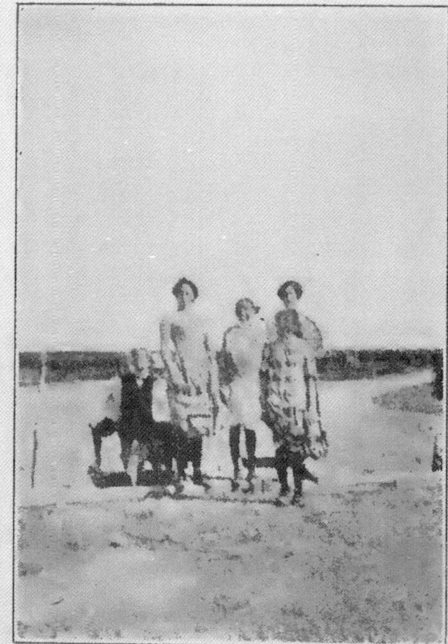

Snake Creek, Going East

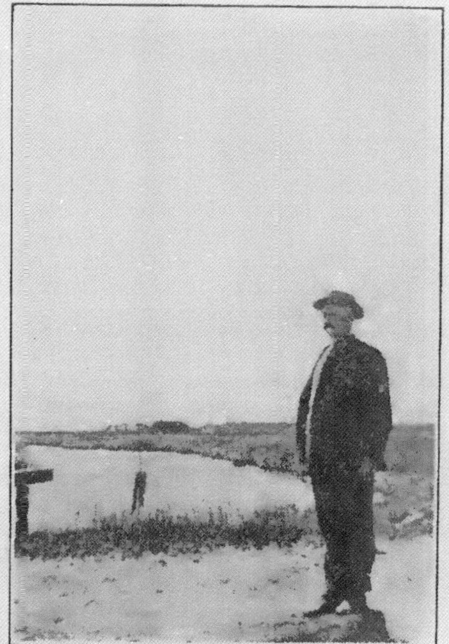

Snake Creek, turn from the south

paying the debt against the church. The punshan (puncheon) of one of those canes will be a relict of by-gone days part of a tree under which King Nummie sat in all his native freedom, surrounded with his tribe and enjoying all the luxuries of the seashore which are so highly prized by us of the present day.

Nummy Town was settled by the whites, but like all other inland places, it has never made much progress, the inhabitants preferring either the bay or the seashore. There is a tradition that Whitefield preached under a big tree at Nummie Town during his sojourn in New Jersey.

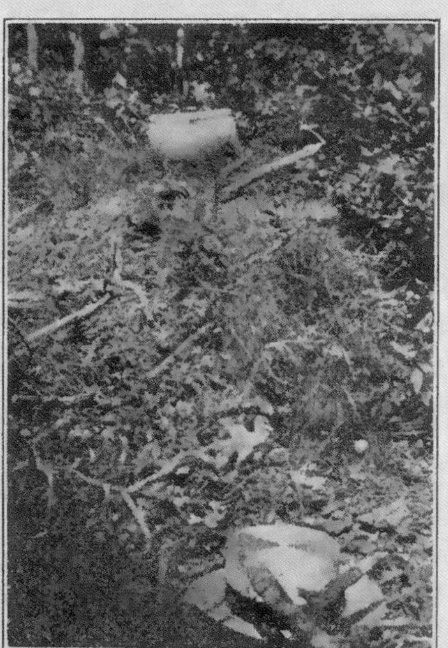

A bank of Cape May Point Ditch. Hat at buttom, stump at top

CHAPTER XII

THE FREEZE TO DEATH YEAR.

The sumer of 1816 is known as the cold summer. There was frost in Cape May County, N. J. every month of the year and so it was through all the settled portions of the United States.. The winter of 1815-16 was an open winter, snow fell in November but scarcely any in December and January. Christmas and New Years were warm, open and green. January was a very mild month, the sun shone every day, people prepared for great storms and cold weather in February, but it was even warmer than January. Near the end of February and the first days of March a terrible storm raged and gave way to cold and boisterous winds. April was like January ending with snow and ice. In May ice formed an inch thick on rivers and streams, buds and flowers were frozen and the entire corn crop was killed. Frost, ice and snow were common in June and all attempts to raise vegetable products failed. Farmers hoarded their crops of the preceding year. Almost every crop was killed and the fruit was nearly all destroyed. July 4th was cold and a blustering wind, raw and uncomfortable, swept the entire Atlantic coast. On the fifth, ice was formed, the thickness of window glass, in New York city and all through New England and in Pennsylvania. It was so cold the Cape May farmers tended their corn the best of which was only about three feet, wearing mittens and coats. In August ice half an inch thick was frequently seen. September and October presented nearer approach to summer weather than any other month of the year. In November extreme cold weather began and a severe winter continued up to April, then summer began and the farmers realized bounteous crops.

While not so severe the same conditions existed in England as in this country, so little corn was raised in this county

that it was necessary to send to the South to get seed corn for the spring planting of 1817. Seed corn from the crop of 1815 brought $4.00 or $5.00 a bushel.

In one ancestral branch of the writer's family food was so scarce that after meals so hungry were the children that they vied with each other to scrape the mushpot for a few specks more to eat. The report comes down that if this family had not owned some valuable cedar swamp that could be converted into cash they would probably have starved to death.

The Star and Wave of May 25, 1912, says:

The year 1816 was known as the "Freeze to Death" year, there being frost every month, and many tales of it have been handed down the generations and are occasionally heard even at this day, 96 years after.

Frank Leaming of Court House, has recently made among some old papers, the discovery of an almanac of that year entitled "Kites Town and Country Almanac, 1816," calculated by William Colborn and printed by Lydia B. Bailey, of Philadelphia. He found it among papers left by the late Dr. Coleman F. Leaming, and supposes it to have been originally owned by Dr. Coleman's father, Jeremiah Leaming to whom he credits the many interesting notations running through its pages, among which are the following: At the bottom of the page for May is the statement "Uncommonly Cold." Opposite May 16, "Frost." From June 7th to 12th "Frost," July 3rd and 4th "Frost," July 29th; "Frost," August 12th, 21st, 29th and 31st, "Frost;" September 3rd, 7th, "Frost," 13th, 14th 15th, 16th, 17th and 20th, "Storm;" September 27th, "Frost;" September 28th, "Storm;" December 4th, "Snow Storm." Another notation states that such a cold year had never before been known by any of the oldest inhabitants. As a result, crops failed and there was a scarcity and high prices which made times very hard. The price of corn rose to $1.75 and $2.00 per bushel and flour to $15 per barrel. No attempt was made to accuse either the Federalist or Democratic party of that day of being responsible for the "high cost of living."

CHAPTER XIII.

INDIAN TRAILS.

The Indian had paths called trails over most of this country. They were around the heads of rivers, or led to fording places where there were shoals, or where the streams were narrow. Sometimes a tree or trees could be fallen so as to aid in crossing. At other places the squaws would carry gravel and build a hard way across the river's bed that at low tide would fall quite or nearly bare and when the tide was not too high could be waded.

These artificial fording places greatly shortened distances as they were usually nearer the mouths of rivers and favored a more direct route while other crossing places led in very circuitous routes.

The white settlers followed these trails. This is why so many old roads are very crooked and also why so many old fields are found near the interior of our county. The whites followed these trails until they came to a stream which stream they would examine for a mill site in conjunction with a good stand of fine cedar and other timber. A great business of our forefathers was shipping lumber to Philadelphia, New York, West India and other ports. These fording places were soon bridged. The trails became roads. Some of them are our roads today. For instance, the road leading from Goshen landing past Swain Station, was an old Indian trail across the county. This is why it is so crooked. It trailed between the swamps or across the narrowest or shoalest places in them. The big bend near Mr. George Gallaher's was built at the narrowest part of what was and even yet is known as Pole Cross Road swamp.

As the whites were able and as business developed bridges were built nearer the mouths of streams. Roads were short-

ened and straightened. The old crooked roads or remains of them around the heads of or between streams were deserted.

At times of migration, war, or battle with the whites, the Indians would often appear or disappear in one direction and reappear in the opposite direction by going and coming over some of these artificial fording places that were secreted from the uninitiated.

CHAPTER XIV.

TORNADOES.

On the morning of August 17, 1876, there appeared in the atmosphere just south of the mouth of Dyers Creek, a cloud having the appearance of smoke. When first seen it was to the naked eye about the size of a quart cup. It kept increasing in size and as it swept in from the bay and over the meadows, a powerful wind from the northwest came with it roaring like several express trains at full speed. From the cloud would run branches, waving and slatting fearfully back and forth in the air, and as it moved in the southeasterly direction it crossed the salt marsh, filling the air with the new mown hay, carrying it nearly all away. Cows feeding in the pasture were blown to the ground.

The tornado moved on crossing the main road destroying the house, barn and outbuildings of the old Pierce's Point farm owned and occupied by Mr. Edward I. Sayre, who with a child in his arms sat talking to his neighbor Wm. S. Leaming. The latter had his head cut and back hurt while getting out. Mr. Sayre with the child (afterward Mrs. Lida Scheutze) rushed out and sat down close to the but of an immense tree about two and one-half feet in diameter, and escaped unhurt. They saw the approaching tempest but did not comprehend their danger nor imagine its severity until it was upon them.

Mrs. Sayre finding the wind coming in at a door, attempted to shut it and at that moment the destructive wind struck the house and she was boxed in between two doors with bricks and fallen timber tumbling all around her. The top of the house off—most of it down—here she was fast but safe for the flooring to the room over her head had sustained the weight of the bricks above and after the storm she was taken out unhurt from a providentially made cell three feet square by seven feet high.

A young man (Mr. Elisha B. Scull) living with Mr. Sayre had just gone into the parlor to try on a new pair of pants, escaped unhurt with his pants but the pants had a big hole through the seat as if a brick had just missed his head and punctured the pants. Three horses that were buried beneath the barn and its contents, were not fatally injured. The buildings were not traps but had been rebuilt the previous spring. The house had two immense chimneys—the old-fashioned fireplace kind which were wrenched into chunks two to three feet in length.

We believe the wind would have destroyed almost any building in this state. Crops were destroyed, corn was stripped of its blades and husks or twisted off close to the ground. Lima beans were shelled; fences blown flat; trees 12 to 18 inches in diameter were uprooted or broken off from two to ten feet above the ground, and some of them stripped of their limbs, others were carried a quarter of a mile in the air without touching the ground; tossing them about as if they had been feathers. Where some struck the ground great holes were dug.

The belt of the tornado was about 200 yards wide and its track for over a mile was marked with pieces of timber, broken boards, shingles, articles of furniture in fragments; clothes hung in trees; barrels, boxes and baskets scattered at random.

The trees in Mr. Wm. S. Leaming's house yard were stripped of many limbs, but the force of the tornado missed by only a few feet his buildings. The wreck and ruin were complete and far beyond the imagination to conceive. Lasting only a few minutes it was over before the community was aware that a calamity had visited them. The day was characterized by thunder showers and some very hard claps of thunder and sharp lightning. The summer had been quite dry and rather warmer than summers here usually are.

PETERSBURG TORNADO.

At Petersburg N. J., July 4, 1881, about 3 P. M., there was a tornado nearly one-fourth of a mile wide of sufficient

force to unroof buildings, blow down three barns, shift buildings from their foundations and blow one store building to pieces.

One tin roof was blown off and rolled up in a bundle. Peter Van Gilder had a horse buried beneath his barn and its contents, when it blew down though it was gotten out without injury.

The storm centered near Mr. James Smith's, passing in a southeasterly direction after demolishing and completely destroying his old apple orchard that contained trees of good size. It spent its force shortly after passing cedar creek. This tornado probably covered a distance of about two miles, being accompanied by rain, hail, thunder and lightning.

UPPER TOWNSHIP TORNADO

At about daybreak October 4, 1849, the occupants of the dwelling standing north of the present Seaside Cemetery and off on the east side of our present boulevard, heard an immense roar of wind passing over the top of their home but so high up as to do them no damage. It came from the southeast and swept down into the hollow near the Lee barn (now owned by Thomas French) twisting one corner of it then crushing one house owned by Samuel Godfrey to the ground and breaking it into fragments without injuring anyone seriously, then as it rose up the hill it carried away the upper half story of Jonas Corson's home, together with his first wife Rachel and her sister who were sleeping in a large room, carrying them eight rods or more. When the wife fell she came down through the limbs of an oak and lodged in it and died soon afterward. The sister, Emma Young, was tossed to one side of the track of the storm and badly hurt, but she finally recovered. The storm here took a northeasterly course. A part of one roof was found in what is now Ocean City.

Mr. Washington Blackman now years old, remembers it well. His father owned the house in which Jonas Corson lived, and had a cornfield in the track of the tornado, the stalks

of which were twisted and crushed to the earth as well as sucked in from the sides. The width of this tornado was only about 25 feet, but it demolished everything in its wake, uprooting trees or breaking them off, destroying crops and hustling dogs, cats, poultry, hay, grass, weeds, bushes and fences in a way unknown to them or their owners before or since.

CHAPTER XV.

THE OLD KING'S HIGHWAY.

At Collingswood the King's highway passed in front of the old Cuthbert mansion which was erected in 1774, which mansion was used as a hospital for colonial troops that passed between Philadelphia and Trenton. It probably passed through the Indian fields near Bridgeton; likely crossed the Maurice River a little to the south of Millville, then through Cumberland on across the head of Manumuskin creek, passing Bennet's mill, Feaster field, on to Tarklin, near where is now located Durell's cranberry bog; also through Beebe field, Sanborn lot, Souder farm, Indian ordinary (usually pronounced "Ornery" because a bad Indian once lived there), Steelmantown, Mt. Pleasant. Hence on south over Long bridge, being the present road that passes the residence of Jehu Bonham (just deceased), the Blenton and Cedar Grove school houses a quarter of a mile east of the present Asbury Methodist Episcopal Church, a little west of the almshouse, and on through Cape May Court House, then bearing to the east going near the meadows in what is now the eastern part of Whitesboro and what was formerly the farm of Amos Cresse near where lie buried since 1807 and 1811 his parents, Philip and Hannah Cresse. It passed in front of the old mill house about half a mile east of Rio Grande on its way south, and I've often wondered if the road leading south over Schellinger's Landing into Cape May City was not its termination. Travel by land from the southern precincts of this county to the Upper was very difficult because of the immense tract of deep swamp extending entirely across the county. Benj. Weatherby of Tuckahoe was told by his mother that so delighted were the inhabitants at the building of this highway that the women voluntarily carried dirt in dishpans to hasten its construction.

Along this old highway can still be seen traces of former homes, black spots of earth, shells, old mortar and bricks. An old cannon ball badly rusted was found in 1913 at Erma near this old route. Before reaching Cape May City it likely passed through what was for many years the fresh banked meadows for which our forefathers seemed to be skilled and famous for making. In many places in this county are traces of old banks for converting salt marsh and swamp in fine fresh meadow. Some banks were built to keep the salt water out of the swamps of cedar

CHAPTER XVI.

JESUS
CHRIST
Is the
Only Key
That
Al-
Ways
Has
Can
Now
And
Al-
Ways
Will
Un-
Lock
The
**PROB-
LEM
OF
LIFE**
Any-
Where
At
Any-
Time
To Any One
Who Carefully
Tests
Him
By
The Principles
Found In The
Holy
Script-
Ures.

CHAPTER XVII.

PLANTS FOR FOOD AND MEDICINE.

Many were the dishes of greens that graced the tables of the early settlers of New Jersey.

Today we eat asparagus, spinach, beet tops, turnip tops, celery, and dandelion leaves as cultivated plants. The housewives of former days gathered from the wilds two to six inches of the tops of poke when it was about a foot high, scalded it pouring off this green poisonous water, boiled and seasoned the poke and had a feast. Others used the leaves and tops of Lamb's quarter, crispus or krinkley dock (sour dock) leaves or a combination of all three, boiling together with a pinch of saleratus for fifteen minutes, then pouring off this first water to get rid of the poison, added a good piece of pork in the second water and furnished a dish fit for a lord.

Doctors know that a few messes of greens in the spring surpass any medicine they can prescribe. Skavish (snake weed) was fine for poultices and would bring a boil to its destination in double quick time.

The root or leaves of the butterfly plant grated and cooked in milk was excellent for scours in calves or for dysentary. Boneset tea (of the leaves) cured "chill and fever." Catnip and hoarhound tea taken hot at bedtime cured colds. Teaberry leaves, spicewood, sassafras root bark, etc., were used in making beer.

Tea of leaves of the gypsum (smart weed) mixed with lard make an excellent salve for the cure of poison from ivy or mangineal (swamp shumac).

Our grandmother's gardens abounded in beds of thyme, sage, fennel, lavender, and they were experts in gathering plants for both food and medicine, catnip, hoarhound, boneset, were dried in quantities for winter use.

The pink flower of the wickie plant easily revealed the

location of the plant that produced a red dye. Then there was the morning star plant with its white top the root of which was made into tea for consumptives, but if a cow had eaten during the day the kill calf plant that usually blooms in July and came up at night frothing at the mouth and acting in a languid manner, she must be given some pork pickle soon or she would die.

Some grandmothers were excellent nurses, almost doctors, and many times both day and night were they called upon and left home, sometimes for days and weeks at a time, the big girl at home taking her mother's place and learned to run a home, managing not only the cooking, but the poultry, the carding, spinning, weaving, the milk, the butter, and the making of the cheese.

Apples, pears, peaches, plums and berries were dried and preserved, furnishing superior and much healthier dishes than do the canned goods of today. Then, too, I would not forget the delicacies when roasted that hung in my grandmother's garret. I almost taste them yet. Japan peas, pop and sugar corn, groundnuts with not far away bushels of walnuts.

In existence today is my grandmother's doctor book—"The Family Adviser by Henry Wilkins, M. D., 1793." Its fourth edition came in 1804, to which was added John Wesley's Primitive Physic. First printed in London in 1747, but the 26th corrected (my grandmother's) edition was printed by John C. Totten, N. Y., for the M. E. Church and sold by Ezekiel Cooper and John Wilson at the Book Room.

In order to show the extent to which our ancestors used plants and their parts, we give a few of the items from said book: For consumption: Boil two handfuls of sorrel in a pint of whey. Strain it and drink a glass twice a day.

For corns: Apply bruised ivy leaves daily and in 15 days they will drop out.

For dropsy: Apply green dock leaves to the joints and soles of the feet, changing them once a day.

For ring-worms: Apply rotten apples or pounded garlic.

For shingles: Drink sea water for a week, toward its close bathe in it or apply pounded garlic.

For a sore mouth: Gargle with the juice of cinquefoil.

For a stitch in the side: Apply treacle spread on a hot toast.

For a venomous sting: Apply the juice of honeysuckle leaves.

For the sting of a wasp: Rub the part with the bruised leaves of house-leek, water cresses or rue; or apply treacle or sweet oil; or bruised onions or garlic.

For sunburn: Wash with sage tea.

For swelled tonsils: Wash them with lavender water.

For warts: Rub them daily with a radish.

For gravel: Eat largely of spinage.

To make the hair grow: Wash every night with a strong decoction of rosemary. Dry it with flannel.

For wounded tendons: Boil comfrey roots to a jelly and apply as a poultice, changing it once a day.

To open a wound that has closed too soon: Apply bruised centaury.

Stone in the kidneys: Boil an ounce of common thistle root and four drachms of licorice in a pint of water. Drink half of it every morning.

Much information in the use of plants they obtained from friendly Indians.

Plots of spearmint, peppermint, dock, plantain, ivy, honeysuckle, and a dozen other plants were kept from year to year and the location of trees and bushes as ash, spice wood, alder, to be quickly obtained in cases of emergency, or in their dyeing and cleansing was carefully noted.

CHAPTER XVIII.

MISSIONARY TO THE LENAPE INDIANS.

These Indians were in general peaceful and New Jersey suffered but little from Indian wars and it is likely that the David spoken of in the following was the agent who saved hundreds of Jersey lives and much property. Indeed we may be living here today because of his influence.

Count Zinzendorf adopted and educated a Moravian peasant lad whom he brought to America to visit his colony at Bethlahem, Pa. He became one of the hardiest and most devoted of the early missionaries. His long wanderings through the wilderness with the Lenape Indians made him their friend and a passionate pity for them filled his heart. His longing to lift them up and make Christians of them was, he believed, a call from God. Count Zinzendorf and his suite, after a lengthy sojourn here, decided to start for home. They were all on their ship in the harbor of New York. It had weighed anchor and was moving down the bay when the Count found David alone on the deck, watching the receding land with tears in his eyes. "Is it possible that you do not wish to go back to Europe?" he asked, for a pleasant and prosperous future awaited the boy there. "No; God bids me go into that wilderness and work for him," cried David. "Go back, then, in God's name!" said Zinzendorf. The ship was brought to and David went back. For sixty-two years he lived with the savages, preaching the gospel to them and never receiving a dollar of salary from any church. David's sacrifice was like that of Joseph, in that it took him far from his home and friends. It is like that of all of us in that it entailed hardships and self-denial in the work of God.

CHAPTER XIX.

WHAT KIND OF A MODEL WILL YOU BE?

Tune:—When the Roll is Called up Yonder.

You are living as a model for the growing girl and boy,
Will you make that life a failure or a joy?
For you will point it up to heaven or down to pain and hell
By the spirit that you let within you dwell.

Chorus:—Oh, keep growing! Always growing!
So keep growing always growing
Oh, keep growing, growing better all the while.

Will you not help hold up to others the good, the pure, the true
So evil may never in their pure souls brew?
For boys smoke and swear and drink and lie because their elders do,
Then let's throw a noble model to their view'.

Chorus:—Then keep growing, always growing,
Then keep growing, always growing,
Then keep growing better all the while.

There are some broken-hearted parents who brought their child up right,
Have seen their dear one switched from the way of light;
And many a struggling weak one has gone the upward track
When they saw a friend in whom was little lack

Chorus:—So keep growing always growing
So keep growing always growing
So keep growing better all the while.

You are serving God or satan and are carrying on the work
Of the one whose spirit you let within you lurk.
Making the next generation one of weakness or of strength,
As you guide those who will view your worth and length.

Chorus:—So keep growing always growing
So keep growing always growing
So keep growing better all the while.

To all that is low or mean or vile, dear child, just shut your eyes.
And elder, show the way to what is good and wise.
Let each one help the other to win our loving Saviour's smile!
Noble then will be the race marching from guile.

Chorus:—So keep growing always growing
So keep growing always growing
So keep growing better all the while.

CHAPTER XX.

THE GREAT SEPTEMBER GALE—1821.

This chapter has for its basis the contributions to the Cape May County Gazette in 1910.

It is fortunate that these typhoons or hurricanes (for this was truly one) rarely reach Cape May. In the West Indies they are generally preceded by a long spell of calm and hot weather. The years 1818-19-20-21 were noted for calms and long continued drought. During the summer a man noted for his reticence but when he did speak it was mostly to the purpose observed, "This summer is very hot, sultry, dry and calm; I think the devil is mending his bellows and will give us a blast before winter." It was prophetic to the letter. The first notice we have of the commencement of this tornado was encountered a little north of St. Thomas, but no doubt originated in the calm latitudes near the equator, caused by the rarification of the atmosphere by extreme calmness and heat. The surrounding cold rushes in from all points to fill the vacuum which produces the rotary motion in comparison to the whirlwind only on a small scale. This tornado traveled north at the rate of forty miles an hour. We may think this an awful ariel phenomenon, but history informs us that it was a small affair in comparison to some others, particularly the one that occurred sixty years before this one.

We read of its striking Norfolk as an immense gale accompanied by flood, rain, rise of tide, and darkness of the heavens. One vessel was found bottom upwards. A hole was cut, a colored woman taken out of the run. The vessel had turned bottom up immediately; all the rest (nine in number) had perished.

Baltimore experienced a great fall of rain with little wind while Philadelphia and New York felt the most tremendous gale that ever visited these parts. The list of damages at New

York filled nearly two columns of a newspaper. Wharves in New York were overflown to the depth of from 12 to 20 inches. Vessels were blown ashore and against each other with great force and badly "stove in" in stems, sides and sterns. Chimneys were blown down and houses unroofed and demolished, while the steeple of a church seemed to rock three feet each way.

At Philadelphia there was havoc among the chimneys and trees. Ten of the fourteen beautiful Lombardy poplars at the Navy Yard were entirely blown up by the roots, and the U. S. vessels driven from their moorings were ship John Adams and frigates Delaware, Guerriere and Congress. One chimney blew over against an adjoining store and when the wind shifted blew back again and stood erect as usual. The water fell in the afternoon to the estimated depth of three and ninety-two one-hundreds inches.

In Cape May County and other places, fields of grain and fruit trees suffered greatly. The force of the wind, says a letter from Egg Harbor, was so great that the spray of the salt water was carried 12 to 14 miles inland, killing vegetation, leaves of trees and herbs. Leaves of orchard trees on the side toward the ocean were turned brown and appeared as if scorched and dead, while on the other side the leaves were green and beautiful.

It has been handed down by tradition in the Townsend family, one noted for truthfulness, that this gale lasted several days. The tides on the marshes were said to have been 12 feet deep. One vessel ashore on the beach was taken over the top of the same and landed in a field between the marsh and the road.

One account reads: "The ocean swept over the beaches along the eastern coast of Cape May County, rushed across the sounds and meadows carrying boats, some with people in them, far up on the mainland."

We think it likely that the seaside suffered about the 3d instant, and the bay side about the 6th, for Mary Blacksom

who became the wife of Barlow Williams, often told her son Charles (now living in Heislerville) that she was born September 6th, 1821, the night of the September gale, when the water of Delaware Bay swept in over the meadows and upland with great force and velocity.

Charles Ludlam, born in South Dennis in 1799 and died there about 1884, wrote: "The morning of September 3d, 1821, commenced with a light wind from the west, there was nothing in the looks of the atmosphere that indicated bad weather. At about 9 o'clock the wind hauled round to the southeast, steadily increasing. At 11 o'clock it might be called a gale, at 12 it was blowing a hurricane with intermittent gusts that drove in doors and windows, blowing down outbuildings, trees, fences and overflowing the marshes between the beach and mainland several feet. At this time it was difficult to stand without some support; no clouds were to be seen, but in their place was a universal haze like a thick fog. The salt spray of the sea was driven inland some miles so as to kill vegetation. At about 10 o'clock it fell perfectly calm for about fifteen minutes, then the wind suddenly burst out from the northwest the directly opposite quarter, and blew with increasing violence for about three hours, then gradually subsided, and by six o'clock had nearly ceased and cleared off at sundown. The evening was as clear as the morning, but oh dire was the devastation it left in its progress. Vessels foundered, driven ashore, or dismasted, woodland nearly ruined by being broken down or blown up by the roots, the writer of this had a favorite weeping willow that made three-quarter of a cord of wood that was blown down by the southeast wind and when it came out, northwest blew it over to the opposite. Cape Island lost from 16 to 20 feet of its bank, and what is most singular, a ship anchored that evening immediately opposite the present breakwater that carried top gallant sails all day and knew nothing of the hurricane. The vortex or center of this cyclone as laid down in Blunt's Coast Pilot, struck our continent at or near the point of the Cape and passed over the center of the county

and could not have exceeded 50 miles in width as it was but partially felt in Bridgeton and Salem. It was a providential circumstance that it was low water and a low run of tides, otherwise it would have been calamitous in the extreme in the loss of life and property.

On our bay shore the tide was higher than on the seaside of the Cape by several feet; persons who witnessed the overflow said it came like a perpendicular wall some five feet high driven by the wind when it changed to the northwest and came in an overwhelming surgle. From the formation of the land in the cove of our bay, in the vicinity of Goshen and Dias Creek and Cedar Hammocks, the water was concentrated as a common center and the tide was higher there than anywhere along the shore; drift was lodged in the tree tops at the Cedar Hammocks nine feet high; in all probability the heave of the sea had something to do in this. What at the time was considered a large coaster was lying at Goshen Landing, broke from her fastenings and brought up in the edge of the swamp near Wm. Garrison Sr.'s. Another vesel at anchor at the mouth of Goshen Creek was dragged with all her ground tackling two miles across meadow and upland and brought up in the middle of the field now owned by Jesse Coombs,(in 1813 by Jesse Winfield Coombs).

In the pasture of Mr. Hugh Hand (owned in 1813 by Geo. Reed and Mrs. Thos. H. Douglass) is a depression or basin of peat soil at the time six feet deep overgrown with alder, maple and other swamp growth, when the overwhelming surge struck and overtopped the hill that intervened between the marsh and the swamp, it tore up the peat soil to the hard pan and rolled it up to the southeast side of the basin like a sheep skin and left a clean pond where before was a peat swamp.

Another says, The September Gale having wrought sad havoc on the Atlantic coast, on September 6th, it jumped out of the northwest and with the tide one-third ebb in Delaware Bay was strong enough to drive it up again, and as old peo-

ple used to say, to two high waters within six hours and a great overflow beside. The top of some of the meadow on the north side of Dyers Creek was skinned off and piled up in a heap where a knoll is to be seen to this day. A sloop boat was deposited in the swamp on the north side of the road leading from Cape May Court House to Dias Creek, near where said road forks about two miles west of the Court House.

Furman Erricson with his seven year old son William, was on the meadows near Delmont seeing the rush of waters approaching, put his son on his back and before they reached the upland the water was nearly to his armpits and he was a tall man.

David High, father of Andrew, Sarah who married John Bench then second a Mr. Feaster, David, Jacob, Ezekiel, Malachi, John and Mary, who married Samuel Errickson, leaving Calvin, Amelia and Mary was at Pierces Point helping to load a vessel with wood. The job completed, he started to walk home as the tide began to rerise. When he reached the main bay shore road one mile from the bay, the tide had come in so fast as to overflow the public highway and soon the waters of the ocean and bay met. This younger Mary's children are the Misses Hattie, Sarah, Helen and Elizabeth Fidler of Dennisville.

Ishmael Armor lived with Jeremiah Ludlam seven years. During the September gale he had occasion to go to the barn on what is now the William S. Thomas place, and found the tide from the ocean running under it. Soon the tide crossed to the farm lately purchased by Clarence McGraw, crossed its field, then on to Siggtown, hence to Mape's mill, thence on down Nancy's creek till it met the water of old Delaware Bay. Ishmael was a truthful, reliable, old trustworthy African, one of the last of Cape May county slaves.

Joseph Ludlam Hand, father of Deborah, the wife of Edward Devaul, Sr., and grandfather and great grandfather of the Devaul's now living at Ocean View, died in the great Sep-

tember gale. His tombstones may be seen at any time on the property then owned by himself.

John Gandy, Sr., who was born in 1802, several times told his son Capt. Francis Gandy, how he himself was on the meadows at the time of the gale and came very near being engulfed by the fast rising tide before reaching the mainland.

Mrs. Eliza Abbett was born in October, 1821. During this gale the roof of their house in Goshen was blown off, and often was she told that then her father carried her mother to the house now occupied by Joseph Kirkbride for safety.

The day of this September gale Elijah Miller lived in the southern end of Dias Creek on the farm now owned and occupied by David Compton. The elements were so threatening that he walked north to the school house and asked for his children, Vincent and Mary. The teacher replied "Can't you stay a little while for we all will be going out soon. But Mr. M. repied, No, I wish my children immediately and advise you to dismiss all the pupils at once and not wait until the regular closing hour." This advice was heeded. One of Mr. M.'s children started to go home a short cut through the woods but as the limbs and tree tops were breaking off, fearing they might be killed thereby, hustled them homeward by the main road as fast as their feet would carry them. Looking back as they went up the hill south of Dyers Creek causeway, they saw great waves capped with foam rolling where they had walked but a few minutes before.

Passing over Connecticut it seemed to leave the continent only to touch New Hampshire by blowing down barns and houses, a child sleeping on a bed, with the bed itself, was carried 150 rods and found dead. A hemlock log 60 feet long and three feet in diameter was raised from the ground and carried six rods.

CHAPTER XXI.

SWEET SIXTEEN.

Miss Sarah Newton, a buxom, healthy Cape May lass of sixteen, lived during the war of 1812 with a family named Edmunds, when the British were in Delaware Bay committing such drepedations as they saw fit. As the British usually came ashore during the daytime to relieve the residents of cattle, sheep, etc., this family reasoned that as they were in need of additional provisions they could lengthen out the supply—in the way that always has been customary in South Jersey—by going fishing, and if they went by night the British would not molest them.

As most of the men were away patroling, guarding, watching and manouvering to outwit the British and protect the country, this young lady and the colored servant girl volunteered to go along and help what they could in hauling the seine and gathering up the fish. Waiting until the hour of midnight to insure safety, they sally forth to Pierces Point, cast the net, bring a good haul to shore, and as they were gathering up the contents thereof, suddenly out of the cedars came the British, taking the fish and capturing these two girls as prisoners.

Miss Sarah and the colored servant were kept for three months on one of the British ships, and while they were well used, they were compelled to act as housekeepers—probably better say shipkeepers. Often when making bread they would knead a whole barrel of flour without stopping.

When the British were ready to sail to other parts, the girls were rowed to shore and given their freedom. August 17, 1815, Sarah was married to James Corson, by Robert Edmunds, justice. Her descendants are living about us today. They were Hetty, who married Moore Douglas (see Chapter XXIV); Jane, who married John Errickson, they moved west;

Mary, who married Jesse Grace; Sarah Ann, who married Richard Ross; Somers Carson, who married Nancy Errickson; James Corson, who married Hettie Conover; and Swain Corson who married Theodocia Corson.

In after years this captive girl is remembered as Aunt Sallie Corson, an excellent nurse among the sick.

Sarah Newton's parents were Nathan Newton who married Rachel Golden. They came from England but were married after coming to America. Her brothers and sisters were Nathaniel Newton, who married Elizabeth Irwin September 21, 1820; Hannah Newton, who married Obed Cresse; Hettie Newton, who married Elihu Barnett; Martha Newton, who married Daniel Cresse. Elizabeth Newton had three husbands —James M. Parsons, married April 19, 1823; Jeremiah Schellinger, father of the late J. Henry Schellinger; Levi Hand, father of Joseph and Elias Hand. Mary Newton married Thomas Taylor, him whom I knew as an old man in 1875, living in Nummytown. Her brothers, Benjamin and Nathan, on a voyage from Philadelphia to New Orleans, disappeared and it was always believed they were captured by pirates. Nathaniel Newton and Elizabeth Irving's children were: Eliza who married Peters Errickson, Rebecca who married Ephriam Sloan; Marie, who married Samuel Sayre; Sarah, who married Levi Hollingshead; Nathaniel Newton and John Newton.

Martha Newton and Daniel Cresse's children were: Abbie, who married Smith Hand; Priscilla who married John Kernan, leaving Abbie, wife of Capt. Leonard Hand; Mary Ann, the first wife of Lieut. Samuel E. Douglass; and John.

Hannah Newton and Obed Cresse's children were Judith, the first wife of John Tomlin; and Eliza, the wife of Joseph Camp, Sr.

CHAPTER XXII.

ALMOST NINETY-FIVE.

MRS. ELIZABETH STITES.

Miss Elizabeth Thompson who became the wife of Captain Adonijah Stites, April 19th, 1839, informs me that she was born July 4th, 1818. Her parents, James Thompson and wife Polly, a daughter of Daniel and Elizabeth Swain, lived near the scene of some doings by the British during the war of 1812, and after the English came into the capes one or more of their vessels came and anchored one-half mile above Fishing creek, outside the bars, off the shore of her late homestead. She further says: "The next morning Capt. Bailey and officers of the British ship came ashore in search of food. My father and my husband's father had gone to drive the cattle to shelter back of the woods so that the British would not discover their whereabouts. Mother and two small children were left alone. She had just put in the spider to bake a loaf of bread, live coals being on the top as well as under the spider, that contained the bread. Then going to the door the British were so near she heard them laugh, and fearing they would burn the house she dashed water on the fire so there would be none convenient for them to use—for it was not so easy to produce fire then with flint and tinder as it is now with matches.

When the older child, Charlotte, was awakened and told that the British were near, so frightened was she that ostrich like, she plunged headlong into a barrel of feathers with her feet sticking straight out above. Hustling her out of that and seizing the baby, James, and the children's clothes in one arm and leading the girl with the other hand to a thick clump of bushes, she hastily put on their garments. Then taking the baby in her arms and the other child by the hand crossed under

and along the worm fence to her grandfather, Richard Thompson's, who lived on his plantation, the farm that now adjoins on its south, the road that runs from Green Creek to Delaware Bay.

Soon after leaving the house she spoke to Capt. Bailey, saying she hoped he was more of a gentleman than to interfere with children and ladies, and that if he took their cattle hoped he would be kind enough to leave them one milch cow so that the children, at least her baby, could have milk.

The British took the sheep. Next morning grand-pop (Richard Thompson, said to be of Irish descent, and who came from Liverpool in 1750) started for the ship. Capt. Bailey gave him four lambs to bring back and asked the privilege of maintaining a brick oven on the shore in which to do their baking. The request being granted, they baked therein for three weeks but for fear that homes would be burned, a sharp lookout was kept by day and a guard stationed at night.

The British burned four sloops in the bay.

Mother lived to be 90 years old, and if God spares me until July 4, 1908, I too, will be 90 years old. How good.

Mrs. Stites was the last survivor of ten children all but two of whom grew to maturity. She lived to be in her 95th year, dying at the Old Ladies' Home, Wissinoming, Philadelphia, Pa., March 5, 1913, and was buried in the Baptist cemetery at Cape May Court House, N. J. The grandfather once built or bought a vessel and named it the James (Jeems & Sary) and Sarah. In after years he or his son Richard or both moved to Cape May Court House and lived in what is now the home of Morgan Hand, Esq., corner of Romney Place and Main St.

Since writing the above I have been told that the people of Fishing Creek neighborhood drove their cattle at this time east on Full Mill road over Full Mill bridge to the north side of Fishing Creek stream, then across Schellinger's run to an island like place partly surrounded by swamp, back and within some tall timber so the British would not find them, to a place in what is now called Green Splinter. Said place where the

cows were kept and guarded was for many days known as the Cow Pen.

Not far from here and about 40 rods east of ex-Senator Robert E. Hand's farm house, used to be a mound that Johnny P. Izard who made his home here before 1850, and for many years afterward, declared to be the grave of King Nummy. Said spot is now hard to find; but Dennis Fisher informs me that it is about half way between the homes of Coleman F. Fisher and Mrs. Joseph Hand under some large cedars. This Full Mill road is the old road that has been lately re-surveyed with a view to having it rebuilt, which would make a direct route from past the Frank E. Bate farm, Fishing Creek to Wildwood, via of Rio Grande.

CHAPTER XXIII.

SKIRMISH AT TOWN BANK.

This article (found by Mr. Frank Leaming in an old book he bought) written in lead pencil and signed "Reuben Townsend," a gentleman of veracity, was handed to me July 10, 1913. I do not know that it has ever been published—Chas. Tomlin.

Skirmish at Town Bank, Cape May County, N. J., during the war of 1812.

He writes: "Allow me to relate to you some of the details of a battle or skirmish that took place at Town Bank, Cape May County, N. J., during the war of 1812.

"As I trust you know Joshua Townsend, my father, was commander in chief of the Cape May brigade during the time that Commodore Barresford had the Delawore bay blockaded by a squadron from the English navy. My father having learned of this blockading squadron had marched his troops down into a beautiful grove about midway from Cold Spring to Town Bank and there encamped. Early one June morning in 1813, a dispatch came from Town Bank stating that gunboats from Barresford's squadron had run a pilot boat on shore at Town Bank and they were purposing as they supposed to come with the armed boats and burn her. The minute men were at once put under "double quick" for Town Bank, finding there a natural fortification back of the sand hills in front of the stranded boat. It was soon noticed that a number of Barresford's gunboats were rapidly approaching the pilot boat. The troops were kept from view until the enemy came so near that the sentinel could see the whites of their eyes. Then the command was given "Take steady aim and fire." Soon it was seen that quite a number of the enemy were killed and a large number wounded.

"The pilot boat was owned by Cape May pilots and was partly loaded with flour and provisions. My father learned afterward from a newspaper sent to him from Holland, that in this skirmish seventeen were killed and many wounded.

"Father soon afterward had occasion to go aboard of Barresford's flag ship with the white flag to exchange prisoners and was treated, he and all his subordinates, with the greatest kindness by the Commodore. The accommodation ladder was richly carpeted and the best wines and refreshments were lavishly furnished.

RUEBEN TOWNSEND
Cape May Court House, N. J.

Note—The above was related to me when a small boy by my father and is no doubt strictly true.

The article further says: "I find that the following persons from Cape May Co. were soldiers in the Revolutionary war: Henry Young Townsend was my grandfather and a captain in 1777; John Townsend, my great-grandfather, was a soldier in the revolution; James Willetts was a captain; Henry Ludlam was fist-lieut. in Captain Townsend's Company; Christopher Ludlam was second-lieut. in Captain Townsend's Company; Joseph Wheaton was second-lieut. in Captain Willetts's Company in 1777; Jacob Cresse was ensign in Captain Townsend's Company; David Hand was ensign in Captain Foster's Company in 1777; Henry Young was ensign in Captain Willett's Company. I also find that Thomas Stites, Humphrey Stites and Henry Stevens were all captains and that Jonathan Jenkins and Salathiel Foster were captains, and that David Edwards was first lieutenant in Capt. Willetts's company; Jonathan Bailey was first-lieut. in Captain Whildin's Company; Jesse Hand was paymaster, Cape May; Memucan Hughes from Cape May was paymaster in 1776, also commissary. Nathan Hand was quartermaster in 1777; Thomas Leaming, Adjutant Cap May Battalion in 1776; Eli Eldridge, first-major Cape May Battalion in 1776; Henry Hand, lieutenant-colonel

Cape May Battalion in 1776; Amos Cresse was lieutenant, and John Cresse captain.

The following persons were privates in the Revolutionary War from Cape May: Robert Campbell, James Godfrey, Hiram Chester, John Golden, Cornelius Corson, Jeremiah Hand, Darius Corson, Japheteh Hand, David Corson, Recompence Hand, Jacob Corson, Jesse Corson, Remington Corson, Parmenus Corson, Nicholas Corson, Levi Corson, Thomas Scott, Amos Willetts, Stephen Young, Uriah Young, all of the above were in Captain Willetts' company.

The State Troops were: David Williams, Moses Errickson, Constantine Hand, Cornelius Hand, David Hand, Eleazer Hand, James Plummer, James Schellinger, David Schull, Richard Vanaman, Lawrence VanHook. Old Moses Griffing was in some company.

Richard Somers, promoted to Colonel, was from Gloucester County, and was the father of Lieutenant Richard Somers a naval officer attached to the Mediterranean squadron of Tripoli, during the Algerian war in 1804, who fitted up the Ketch Intrepid that was blown up. He and all on board perished.

Nicholas Keen was captain of the armed boat Friendship. Hope Willetts was captain of the privateer Black Jack during the Revolution.

CHAPTER XXIV

DOUGLASS.

Says the "Newark Evening News" of June 15, 1912: "On a building on South Broad Street, (Trenton, N. J.) erected where formerly the Douglass house stood, the following legend appears: "Here in the house of Alexander Douglass, Washington called a council of war on the evening of January 2nd, 1777, when the flank movement to Princeton was decided upon." Erected by the Trenton High School Class of 1903, on February 22nd, 1902.

This Alexander Douglass, a revolutionary hero patriot, lived to the age of 115 years.

The N. J. States Prison now stands on a portion of what was once Alexander Douglass's farm. He sold it for what was believed, at that time, to be a big price but soon after the sale the value of the Continental money depreciated so greatly that what he received for the large farm was almost nothing. He surely knew the value of the expression "not worth a continental".

About 1800 Thomas Douglass, a son of the above named Alexander, migrated to Cape May County and settled first on what is now known as the Douglass field, which is a little to the south of the old Tick Neck farm, two miles west of the Cape May Court House.

January 25th, 1792 he, Thomas Douglass, of Burlington buys of George Hand, of Cape May, in the Middle Precinct on the Bay side, 270 acres of land for 400 pounds in gold or silver. Quit claims had been given from Absalom and John Hand to George Hand when the land had been sold to him by the sheriff from Benjamin Taylor to whom it had been conveyed by Memucan Hughes who had bought it of Neri Hand who had heired it from his father Thomas Hand.

This Thomas Douglass, I, died October 26th, 1805, age about 50 years. His tombstone stands in the Baptist cemetery at Cape May Court House, N. J., but his body lies buried near the north line of that 270 acre tract in the northen end of the village of Dias Creek, N. J., on an elevation at the west of a turn in the public highway, that is a little to the south of the road that leads to the Cedar Hammocks where once were located two adjoining family burying grounds, those of John Hand and Thomas Douglass.

This Thomas Douglass, I, had a wife Keziah. They left eight children: John, William, Joseph, Thomas II, Nancy or perhaps Nancy Ann, Sarah, Eleanor and Keziah.

1. John Douglass, a lieutenant, married Lydia Norbury (sister of Heath) September 16th, 1804. They left Lydia who married John Fox. Another daughter married and left a daughter Mary who married a Mr. Stetzer. John married (2) Mary Dickinson December 24th, 1809 (a doctor's daughter). John married (3) Rachel Hewitt May 1st, 1811. She bore him John who married Cornelia Crawford; Shamgar who married Clarissa Eldredge; Sarah who married Benjamin Springer; Maria who married Reuben Stephens; Eliza who married William S. Leaming; Enoch who married Mary Ann ——; Rachel who married Martin Clark, and Nathaniel who married Emma Foster.

2 William Douglass (known in my day as Uncle Billy) was about 17 years of age when he came with his father's family as it moved to Cape May County. He, by trade, was a ship carpenter and at one time in his life built vessels on Sluice Creek and lived at Dias Creek on his plantation (now the Michael Cook farm is a portion of it), walking to and from his work.

He it was who advised planting Quaker guns (gum logs shaped and painted to resemble cannon) from the Cedar Hammocks southward along the Delaware shore in 1812 to frighten off the British when they sailed into the bay so that the British

would not seize cattle and commit depredations as they were doing in other places. The ruse was successful.

William Douglass married three times. First Mary Izard (July 3, 1809) by whom he had Thomas, II, who married Elizabeth Eldredge, December 27, 1838, and William, II, who married Sophia Hildreth January 15, 1840; and Judith, the first wife of Nathaniel Norton, and Marcy who died unmarried January 15, 1837, aged 27 years. This wife, Mary, dying October 24, 1824, he married December 5, 1825, Deborah Hildreth, April 9, 1828. Achsah Hand became his last wife, she died November 6, 1873, in her 74th year. He died March 9, 1869, in his 86th year. They left Rebecca, who married Franklin Ludlam, who left Franklin and Emma. Deborah H. who married Thomas Sayre; Ann F. who married George W. Benezett, and Joseph, who married Mary Garretson.

Joseph Douglass married Mary Golden July 3, 1809, left Betsey Ann Douglass who married (1) Iran Curtis, and (2) Nathaniel Edwards.

Thomas Douglass II (Uncle Tommy) who was a patrolman of the Delaware bay shore in the war of 1812, married twice. 1st, May 31, 1812, he married Rebecca Hand. She left Achsah, who married Shamgar Hewitt; Recompence, who married Mary Hand; Amos, who married Elizabeth Bush; Moore, who married Hetty Corson; Alexander, who married Matilda Smith; Page, who married first Ruth Norton, 2d, Kate Silvers, nee Finley, 3d, Sarah ——. Uncle Tommy's second wife was Eliza Stites, whom he married August 15, 1835. She left Hannah, who married Frank Cornwell, and Keziah, who married Joshua Robinson.

Nancy Douglass married Anthony Smith, February 22, 1810. In after years they moved to the west. Nancy once on horseback with a child in front of her going from their home which joined Nancy's creek (now often called Bidwell's) on the north to that of her father's, nearly a mile to the south fell through the bridge, horse, child and herself, and came very near being drowned, but David Patterson in time came to

their rescue and by much effort saved them all, but to this day the name Nancy's applies to the bridge and stream between the villages of Goshen and Dias Creek, because of said accident, the main cause of which was a very high tide. The causeway across the meadow here was raised a few years ago, but before that the tide has several times in the writer's lifetime, been covered with tide water to a depth of from two to four feet. It is said that the man who contracted to build the first road across here became financially wrecked because of the immense quantity of material it took to fill it; there seemed to be no bottom thereto.

Sarah Douglass married Harvey Shaw February 14, 1815.

Eleanor, or Ellen, Douglass married Joseph Foster (school teacher) January 30, 1817, and left Keziah who married Steelman Robinson, and Ellen, who died unmarried, at a good ripe age. Joseph Foster was Dutch, and Ellen, his wife, is said to have had some Welsh blood, Keziah and Steelman Robinson left Douglass J., who married Jane James, and Ada, who married Samuel Earl. They have Elmer, Reed, Curtis, Leslie, Lewis, Lena who married a Mr. Zimmerman, Samuel, Evelyn, Edith and Charlotte.

Keziah Douglass married Charles Wible and moved to the west

John Douglass and Cornelia Crawford's children are: Eleazer Douglass, who married Josephine Allen, leaving Carrie and John who married Edna Swain, and Arabella Douglass who married Harry Corson. Their children are Bessie that married Ferdenand Witt, Cora, Burton D. that married Lyda Springer, whose child is named James Burton; and Harry.

Shamgar Douglass and Clarissa Eldredge's children are Lewis H., who married Sallie Fidler, leaving Clara who married Osmond Geary, and Phebe who married Leon Grace. Leslie married Mary Hall, leaving Percy, Josephine, Harold, May, Lula, Clara and Roxana (Annie) E. married George

Eldredge, leaving Lewis, Allen and Cora who married Reed Chambers.

Allen Douglass, living today on the portion of that 270 acre tract which when divided was set off to John Douglass I, Allen lives with his mother Clarissa, who is quite active at the age of 83 (Oct. 24, 1913) years. A refined, clear-minded lady whom to know is to love. The one and a half story part of the house in which they live and the one and a half story of the first house to the south that is on the opposite side of the road, were formerly one and stood a little to the south of this one near the two big pear trees, for when the property was divided, a brother each took one-half of the homestead with his share of the land and each built a two story and a garret to the part taken. A walnut cupboard eight feet high four feet wide twenty inches deep stands in this home. It was brought to Cape May when Thomas Douglass I moved here from Trenton, N. J.

John Douglass married Hattie Rice.

Shamgar H. Douglass, a railroad conductor on some steam railroad near Salt Lake City, Utah..

Sarah Douglass and Benjamin Springer's children were: Jesse, who married Emma Shropshire and left Wilburt, who married Carrie Garrison leaving Charles and Emma; and Mamie married Charles Mixner and left Jesse, Keziah, Hannah who married Frank Wallace; Benjamin Franklin who married Mrs. Mary Townsend nee Tomlin. They left Frank, May, Marcus, Clara.

Mariah Douglass and Reuben Stephens' children are: Charles, Amassa, Adaline, Elizabeth, Lydia, Anzineta.

Eliza Douglass and William S. Leaming's children were: John D., Furman, Edward, Cassie, Pennington, Bennington, Emma, Lizzie.

Enoch Douglass and Mary Ann's children are Rachel, Millie, William, Charles.

Rachel Douglass and Martin Clark's children are John, Robert, Cora and Rachel.

Nathaniel Douglass and Emma Foster's children are Shamgar who married Mary Schellinger; Emma Jane and Ada.

Thomas Douglass and Elizabeth Eldredge's children are Samuel E. (a lieutenane in the Civil War) married Mary Ann Kernan, of whom is Dr. John Douglass who married Edna Collins, and Francis Douglass who married Achsah Hand, leaving Thomas Holmes Douglass who married Emma C. Tomlin, having Holmes Tomlin Douglas, Francis Douglas, Jr. Mary Emma who died age one week, Samuel Townsend Douglass. Augusta who married Wilbert F. Bateman leaving Fannie, Harvey and Mary. Percey L. married Mamie Norton; they have Robert Stanley and John Warmuth.

H. Freeman Douglass married Josephine Schellinger; she left George who married Jennie Smith, leaving Mary, Donald, Wallace, Cathaline, Margaret. Belford married Alice Beatrice Boyd, leaving Josephine, Alice May, Freeman. Nelda married Charles Ginder, leaving Douglass and Wilbert. Hannah. Howard Douglass married Maggie Bingham. Thomas Reeves Douglass married Annie Powell. Mary Isard Douglass married Burton Lee Howell, leaving Elwood who married Bertha Norton, leaving Edna, Raymond(who was drowned), Beatrice, Leroy, Burton, Howard, Norman. Clarence who married Melicent Tomlin, they have Esther Ruth.

William Douglass and Sophie Hildreth's child was William H. Douglass who married Eliza Gandy, and they left a son Walter E. Douglass who married Hattie Garrison whose child is named Ethel.

Deborah H. Douglass who married Thomas Sayre left Mary who married William Garretson a son of Nelson and Eliza. They have one daughter Alice who married Joseph P. Mackissic, their children are J. Fred., William G., Anna Katherine, Nelson G., Mary G. Dr. Jeremiah E. Sayre who married Lizzie ——, their children are Charles, Wm. Edith, Annie B. Sayre who married Rev. James B. Shaw and they left Walter Y. who married Elsie Hand, who left J. Clinton and Ellen

H. William D. Sayre who died when a young man unmarried Rebecca Douglass who married Franklin Ludlam left Franklin, Emma and Achsah who died young.

Ann F. Douglass married George W. Benezett; their children are Laura S. who married Township Clerk A. T. D. Howell, and Mary Ella who married Capt. Charles P. Vanaman our late surrogate. They have one son, Stanford.

Joseph Douglass married Mary Garretson daughter of Nelson and Eliza, they left Judge Harry S. Douglass whose first wife was Eleutheria Smith, his second, Marion Wheaton who left Wheaton Douglass and John Branin Douglass, his third, Mrs. Hattie Edwards nee Smith. Theresa Douglas who married Daniel W. Kendall. Nelson G. Douglass who married Adella Mason leaving Nelson Granville, Gideon and Theresa Isabel. Gideon Douglass. Eliza Douglass married Capt. Robert Thompson, Jr. Joseph Douglass married Hannah Stiles, they have Charles who married Eloise Valiant, Herbert S., Olive, George, Joseph.

Achsah Douglass and Shamgar Hewitt left Rebecca D. who married Elmer Willets, they left Shamgar, Eva who married Harry Tuttle leaving Edward, Elmer, Horace, Charles. Achsah married Alexander Schellinger and left Rita.

Recompence Douglass married Mary Hand and left Emma Jane who married George Ramsbottom, Amos, Rachel who married James Muncey leaving Freeman, William Clements, Mary who married George Taylor leaving Walter. Freeman, Lizzie who married Mr. Robertson, Rebecca married George Roberts leaving a son George. Amos Douglass married Elizabeth Bush. Moore Douglass married Hettie Corson and left Ellen who married Robert Errickson, they left Deborah who married J. Clement Foster leaving Roy, Frances Celestine, Arthur Everett. Hettie who married Frank Nichols, leaving Erma who married Edward Taylor; Marion and Boyd. Robert who married Anna Gandy leaving Florence. Caroline who married Stacy Tyler leaving William J. who married Mary H. Holmes leaving William Boyd. Susan C.

who married Charles R. Holmes leaving Charles Wendell and Mildred Caroline. Lydia who married Lemuel Thurston leaving Charles, Benjamin, Martha, Lemuel and J. Willets. Laura who married Elmer Cox leaving Alexander, Ralph, Elmer and Douglass. Alexander who married Malinda Smith that died June 7, 1913, leaving Edgar who married Marietta Stites who left Etta and Nora. Alexander who married first Abigail Cresse, 2d Maud Hand who left Georgiana May. Malinda M. who married David McPherson leaving Mildred Irene, Edgar Stanley and Frank Bate. George Anna who married 1st, Joseph Heritage leaving Justin who married C. Edward Hughes leaving Walter (2) Thompson Fennimore Justina.

Page Douglass married Ruth Norton (1), they had Thomas, Orrin, Theodore, James, Rebecca who married Edward Wheaton and left Fannie, Monroe, Keziah, Frank, Ruth, (2) Page Douglas married Kate Silvers, 3d Sarah ——. Hannah Douglass married Frank Cornwell and left Sallie, Lida, Frank, Lot, Tillie, Charles. Keziah Douglass married (1) Joshua Robinson who left Nula; Keziah Douglass married (2) Mr. Parsons.

CHAPTER XXV.

A HEROINE.—WHERE I'D LIVE.—OUR ALBINO

Miss Augusta Willets, now the wife of Dr. Charles E. Edwards, and a daughter of Dr. Reuben Willets and Hannah Brick, writes:

John Willets (my great great grandfather) came from Wales and settled at Willets Point, Cape May County, N. J.

My great grandfather, James Willets, lived at Beesley's Point and had five sons, all taking an active part in the American Revolution, except my grandfather Nicholas, who at that time was too young. James Willets married Rebecca the daughter of Nicholas Stillwell. She was a great Whig during the war of the Revolution, and a bit of history is connected with her as a heroine.

When left alone one day and being, as was the usual custom of all the settlers, on the lookout, while using the spyglass she discovered an armed barge in the bay filled with red coats. Soon they were seen rowing straight for her house.

The cannon already loaded, stood on the river's bank; on came the British and when they were within one-half mile of the Beesley's Point Hotel (bought of Mr. Golding by Nicholas Stillwell in 1750) she ran up the Stars and Stripes. She then hastened for and returning with a firebrand fired off the cannon. The grape shot was seen to fall thickly around the boat. The men fell flat. Soon the boat turned and put to sea. How many were killed or wounded or what became of the boat was never known. Their property and perhaps her life was saved by her daring act. She lies buried in the Stillwell burying ground at Beesley's point.

Mother also used to tell about the British stopping at great-grandmother Elfreth's, near Haddonfield, and stealing money and also some silver spoons that were hidden in an old clock.

WHERE I'D LIVE.

Let me live in the home where it's glad mistress sings
Let me live in the home where the boy's whistle rings
Let me live in the town where the choir's up to date
And can furnish a sweet singing girl for my mate.

Let me work in the place that's lighted by the sun
Let me work with the friend who in his work finds fun
Let me go to the Church where they sing from the heart
And the instrument's music is drowned from the start.

Let me strive for the home of the good and the blest
Let me live for the land where my soul shall find rest
Let me live so that others may find their way there
And bask in the pure realms of God's diadems fair.

OUR ALBINO.

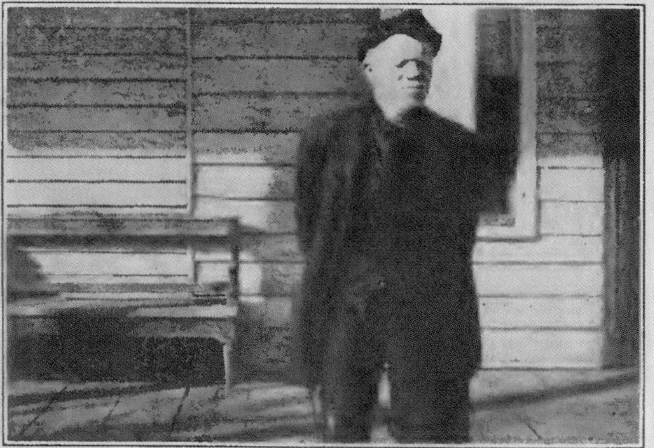

Samuel Humphries

Notice the picture of Samuel Humphries (an Albino) the only one living in Cape May County.

Webster says: "An Albino is any person of preternatural whiteness of the skin and hair, and a peculiar redness of the

iris and pupil of the eye. The term was originally applied by the Portuguese to the white Negroes they met with on the coast of Africa."

Samuel, born of colored parents at Cold Spring in 1839, is the son of Peter Humphries and his wife Kezia Coachman. Samuel's sister Ann Maria, died unmarried many years ago.

Another sister Hester (Hetty) Humphries, married Benjamin Obekiah, and they had three children, Benjamin, Jr., William and Kezia who married James Brown, a carpenter. They have a child named Frances.

Hester was born in 1835 and died in 1906. She, Samuel and Ann Maria were all Albinos, but no other descendant has turned out to be so. How many Albinos are there in New Jersey? How many in the United States?

CHAPTER XXVI.

A PRISONER IN DIXIE.

The article by Samuel Springer, Esq. (who died in 1877), is today, July 10, 1913, in my possession loaned to me by his daughters. We think it has never been printed before although dated December 9, 1867, and said to be written for Foster's War History of New Jersey.—Chas. Tomlin.

At the beginning of the war with Great Britain in 1812, I was 12 years of age. My father, Jesse Springer, was an officer in the militia, and during that war was actively engaged in the defence of our County against the repeated attacks on the shore, mostly made for plunder, such as carrying off stock, etc., by the enemy from their ships of war lying in the mouth of Delaware Bay. During those alarms my business was to issue arms as they came for them taking their names and then to see that they were safely returned when the alarm was over. Those arms were furnished by the state. The last year of the war being then in my fifteenth year, I joined the first artillery company of Cape May under Captain Furman Leaming. At the age of 22 I was appointed captain of that company and continued with the militia until disbanded, I think about 1828.

Thus what I saw of the war of 1812 and my connection with a volunteer company of artillery, gave me somewhat of a military spirit which has never left me. At the breaking out of the rebellion of 1861, it was thought by many that New Jersey might become the battlefield, it being a border state, and our County being in sight of the slave state of Delaware, we naturally began to look around to see what means there was for defence, and soon discovered they were poor indeed.

My grandfather, Samuel Springer, served during the Revolutionary war and was a commissioned officer for the New Jersey line and fought under General Washington.

At a meeting held at the Court House, I was appointed with

a number of others to call together those who were able to bear arms. But the thing did not seem to take and it was abandoned, especially when we found the rebels could not take Washington and that the war was likely to be confined to the line of the Potomac. Some of the young men in my immediate neighborhood caught the fire and requested that I would form them into a company which was done and they continued to drill once a week until the call was made for the nine months men, when the foremost of them joined the regiment and served out the time of their enlistment, with credit to themselves and an honor to their county and state. Several of them re-enlisted and served during the war.

I have written the above mostly as an introduction to my experience in the great rebellion before it was brought to a close.

As the war progressed and often looked dark indeed, I did what I could in the way of encouragement, both by precept and example, and nothing kept me from entering the service but the weight of years. I was offered the captaincy of a company that was being raised but declined for fear that I might be in the way of some one who was better able to bear the hardships and trials of a campaign.

I was appointed Deputy Provost Marshal by Colonel Johnson and served for a while in that capacity to the best of my ability. As the war went on I was alive and anxious for victory to crown as it eventually did, the great struggle for the life of the nation.

In February, 1865, I received an appointment from Captain Kimble, A. Q. M., at Newbern, N. C., to take charge of a detail of men for the purpose of raising some of the many sunken vessels in the vicinity of Newbern and its adjacent waters. I acordingly proceeded hither and reported for duty the 10th of March, 1865. During that month I was employed in making preparation for the prosecution of the business I was appointed to perform. On the second day of April I received written instructions to proceed the next morning on

a steamer which was going up the Neuse river. This boat was to carry me with 22 negroes to a barge that had been sunk by being towed up the river. These vessels with a great number of others were engaged in carrying supplies to General Sherman's army which was then at Kenston. We proceeded accordingly and was put on board the wreck 20 miles from Newbern April 3d, at 12 o'clock. There was some talk that the Rebs were prowling about on the north side of the river. But as the man who had charge of the wreck had been there ten days, had neither seen nor heard any enemy, I did not apprehend any danger so proceeded to enter upon the work I was sent to accomplish.

The steamer having gone on up the river, I together with the captain of the barge and the darkies were left to prosecute our work and be ready to go back the next day with the steamer on her return. We passed the day and night without seeing any one or hearing anything to disturb us except an occasional screech or hoot owl which sounded quite omnious as it came booming through the cypress and the pines which are the growth of the swamps that border the river on the north side that being the side on which the wreck lay. Tuesday morning, April 4, the sun rose clear and beautiful; we ate our breakfast and all seemed going on well. We thought the steamer would be along about noon. By ten o'clock we had finished up our work and was sauntering about some on the barge, others on the banks, when of a sudden, like a clap of thunder from a clear sky came the report of a dozen rifles, some of the balls coming so near their sound was anything but pleasant. I was sitting on the after part of the boat and looking up saw them reloading their pieces; of course there was nothing to do but surrender, and I accordingly did so. Some of the men jumped overboard and were swimming for the other shore. I told them they had better return, fearing they would be shot, so they returned.

The rebels had come down an old road which struck the river at a short distance above where we were, and then crept

along through the swamp behind the big trees which stood thick on the banks of the river. One of the darkies was captured and they compelled him to tell all about who we were. They knew we had no means of defence hence the firing must have been to gratify that desire the rebels have manifested during the whole of the rebellion, to let no opportunity slip to kill a Yankee.

They were twelve in number, headed by their captain with his orderly sergeant. After having secured the negroes that were on the shore, they jumped on board of a plank from the shore to the boat. The captain came to me and ordered me on shore. I, not thinking it worth while to be in such a great hurry, he informed me if I did not move faster that he would knock my brains out. Thinking by that means to put me on the double quick. I however was still a little sulky and slow which caused me to get several broad hints and that in not the most polite manner either.

They seemed to be in the greatest hurry imaginable, so much so that they left considerable plunder they might otherwise have saved. I afterward learned that they were afraid that their firing might attract some of our gunboats, two or three of which were patrolling the river. They, however, soon gathered up what they found, set fire to the barge and started us on a march through the swamp and then 22 miles to the camp at Greenville. The first third of a mile was over an old tressle work where the water was waistband deep, and many were the curses and threats the poor negroes got if they wet the luggage they were carrying. At length we reached the solid ground and being out of the reach of the gunboats, the word was given to halt. Then came an overhauling of the plunder and search for more. Thinking I might possibly have something about me they had not yet seen, I was ordered to turn my pockets inside out. They found to their delight, some articles that they thought might be of use to them. Indeed it would seem as if there was nothing but what they stood in need of from a needle to a steam engine. They

however took all they could find about us, although not of large amount yet more than I liked them to have. If I could have helped it.

In my pockets they found pocket-rule, pencil, knife, memorandum book, twelve dollars in greenbacks. In my carpet-bag a full suit of clothes I had brought with me for a change in case I got wet. They also got from me two new United States blankets, umbrella, etc., amounting in value to over $100. They took nothing from me I had on, that was reserved for another picking. This through with, we were ordered forward, so we passed along. In passing a house we saw some females cheering and making demonstrations of joy at our expense. About ten o'clock we met a company of rebel soldiers going down the road. This squad I afterward learned reached the river three or four miles below where we were captured and burned two steamboats and several schooners. The men on board of one of them showed fight, for this they were taken on shore and hanged. About four o'clock we halted at a farmhouse. The captain and his sergeant went in and ordered dinner, after which myself and the Irishman, the captain of the barge, were invited in and seated at the table. I did not feel much like eating, my thoughts were too busy trying to penetrate the future and see when all this would end, and I must confess the more I tried to penetrate the future the darker it looked. Here I was a prisoner among the rebels, the very name of which had become a terror throughout the land. The thought of the news of my capture reaching my wife and children, everything uncertain to them as to what had or would become of me, was well calculated to give one feelings of not the most agreeable kind. At any rate I did not feel like eating a very hearty dinner, but was somewhat amused with the old farmer, a man of some 60 years in addressing the sargeant he said: "I have always been opposed to the war, and have said we should be whipped, and I still believe so." The sargeant said: "Oh, no; you'll see, said the farmer, and that before long too. Why here is Sherman now at Kenston," and

I am looking for some of his men down this way every day and they'll skin you out of your boots." I began almost to tremble for the old patrot for fear they would take him up for a traitor to their cause.

After dinner we proceeded on our march reaching Greenville an hour after dark. There was no small stir among the rebs on our arrival. All wanting to know where we were from, where we were captured, what we were doing, and a thousand questions more.

There was one circumstance which occurred during our march which I think worth mentioning. The white man that was captured with me was in the employ of the government, receiving good pay and at times was entrusted with the care of supplies to a large amount, yet that man at the first opportunity he got to speak with the captain commenced in this style: "I wish this d—d war was over; I was always opposed to it; nothing but a d—d nigger war and ought to be stopped," and a great deal more of the same kind of talk. I felt like kicking him but thought it best to say nothing. The rebs listened to his palaver but I do not think he made very great impression in his favor, certain it was he had none shown him. There is no doubt but there was too much of such talk as that by many of our men who came in contact with the rebels, all of which helped to encourage them and prolong the struggle. When we arrived in camp we were shown the ground we were to occupy during the night; nothing said about rations, although the negroes had had nothing to eat since breakfast. I lay down under a large pine tree, the root of which served for a pillow. The night passed and morning came which only brought with it a more keen realization of our condition.

They gave us some corn cake and a little bacon for our morning meal, which would have been relished by the darkies had there been three-quarters more of it in quantity. The adjutant of the regiment seemed to be an officer who had not lost all feeling for humanity, gave pen, ink and paper and I wrote two letters in hopes they might find their way through the

line which they never did until Johnson surrendered. About eight o'clock we were put in charge of four mounted men with two revolvers each and started on a march of thirty miles for Tarborough. About twelve o'clock we passed a company of rebel cavalry; they were dismounted and their horses were browsing through the bushes. Nothing special occurred during our march unless it was the taking from me a new pair of water boots and cutting the buttons from my coat which they said they wanted for making finger rings. In exchange for the boots they gave me an old pair of shoes more than an inch too short. I had to cut the uppers all out at the toe so as to let my foot out so as to get them on. After a long, weary journey under a hot sun, and over a sandy road, at length reached our destination tired and footsore, glad to lie down in any place they would permit. That night we were put in prison, and a filthy place it was. The negroes were put in an ordinary room and some of their owners came to see them. Loud were the curses and threats which we could plainly hear. I saw them no more until my return to Newbern, when I met most of them rejoicing in their freedom. The next day we were put on the cars for Wellden; as we were getting on the cars I saw a colored woman, with some boiled shad and corn cake, having had nothing to eat since the morning before, I called her to me, she asked three dollars for a lunch, I purchased two, one of which I gave the Irishman and paid her out of the money my capturers gave me for the green backs they took, remarking, at the time, they did not want a man's money for nothing. The fish and cakes were excellent and were the only good victuals I had while a prisoner. The cars started and we soon arrived at a station on the Wilmington and Wellden R. R., called Rocky Mount, here we were put off for some two hours. At this place a man they called Doctor, did not learn his name and glad I did not. Being told who we were, he said we ought to be hung on the spot, said men that were soldiers had been forced into the service which he seemed to think was the case with all our troops. They were deserving and ought

to have some mercy shown them, but civilians who would engage in carrying supplies to Sherman's army ought to be hung. But it ended in talk and we were permitted to pass the first tree without being hung while the doctor was ventilating himself. Then came a car in from Richmond bringing news that General Grant had captured Richmond, but as they said the man was a notorious liar they professed not to believe it. I heard the man's story and made up my mind it was true. He said when he left they were carrying papers by cart loads into the street in front of the capital where they were being burned What a tale those papers and documents might have told could they have been saved. We soon started for Wellden where we arrived a little after sunset. Here we were brought before the Hon. the Rebel Pro'v. Mar. and subjected to another search and robbery. By this time I had ripped the seams in the legs of my pants and in the sleeves of my coat by which means I saved them. They however took what they wanted even the balance of the rebel currency that was on me, I thought that was a little too mean even for a rebel. That night we were put in what they called a guardhouse and furnished with corn cake and raw bacon, being the third meal they had furnished us up to the evening of the third day after our capture. That evening we had an addition of three to our number, two from Grant's and one from Sherman's. The one from Sherman's army was stripped of every thing except his shirt and pants and the poor fellow was shivering with the cold. He was from Ohio and had been with Sherman during the long campaign through Georgia.

The next day came news that a strong force from Grant's army was advancing and the whole place was thrown into a terrible commotion. There were some rebel soldiers in the place, but to make any resistance seemed to be the last thing thought of. They hurried off their artillery to a place of safety, filled the long bridge over the Roanoke with turpentine so that it might burn quickly when a match was applied and made every preparation to get away as fast as possible. I

began almost to hope they might, in their hurry and great perplexity, forget us so we might probably escape. We stayed there two days during which time the upper bridge was burned and I understood the lower one the day after we left. We were put on the cars and started for R. (likely Raleigh), the cars were full of rebs fleeing, in the seat near me was a Virginian, a member of the legislature, of course all the conversation was about the war. Richmond was captured, but that was nothing, it should have been given up long ago, now they were free to act, did not have Richmond to defend, General Lee would fall back to the mountains and carry on the war to an indefinite period. The legislative man in speaking of the probability of the war being brought to a close remarked there was little chance of that as one of the conditions that were exacted by the North was that the South should pay the whole expense of the war. This was news to me, I thought I was fairly well posted in the leading questions bearing on the subject and I had never heard such a thing mentioned, so I told him that I did not believe such a thing had ever entered the minds of any of our statesmen; at any rate I was certain that it had never been made public. But he seemed firmly to believe it. I suppose it was promulgated by the rebel leaders in order to make the people of the South more bitter and so prolong the war. One tall, lank and lean fellow, evidently one of the poor white trash but who no doubt thought he was of some importance, accosted me thus: "What does yorn come down here to fight mens for, if you stay at home mens will not go to fight yorn" I told him the North were trying to save the South from their own folly. We arrived at R. (likely Raleigh) after dark and turned into the prison pen without a thing to eat. The night was a stormy one, and not the least kind of a shelter, so I passed the night without lying down. In the pen were some 30 or 40 prisoners and the next morning we had an addition of some 15 more. These men were all captured by being sent out from Sherman's army to relieve the necessities and destitution of many of the inhabitants who were in a starving con-

dition rendered so mostly by being plundered by the rebel army. Next day we were subjected to another search when they took from us anything of any value and gave us their filthy rags in return. After this they issued some rations as they called it, which consisted of a double handfull of corn and cod meal, a piece of bacon the size of your two fingers, some of it nearly rotten at that. This was for 24 hours. When we were called up, woe be to the fellow who had nothing to put it in. Some used their shoes, some their hats if they were lucky enough to have one. Thus in various ways the scanty meal was secured. Then the thing was to cook it; we were provided with no kind of cooking utensils whatever, and all kinds of methods were resorted to in order to get the stuff so it could be eaten at all. The meat we could put on a sharp stick and poke it in the fire, but to bake the cake was the thing and the result with me was I lost all realish for food. Having always been used to good clean food and plenty of it, but at such as this my stomach revolted, and I was scarcely hungry at any time during my captivity. During our stay here, which was four days, there were some acts of cruelty by the rebs towards some of our men.

A young man by the name of Scott, for the alleged offence of using some unbecoming language towards the ladies of the South, was tried and found guilty and the court decided the offence was one that would warrant his being shot, but their tender mercies moved them to commute the sentence and he was brought into the pen, gagged and what they called busked. This was tying his hands together, making him sit on the ground with his tied hands locked over his knees, utterly unable to move in any direction. He was compelled to remain in this painful position from 9 o'clock A. M. till 5 P. M., when he was released with the admonition that he was under great obligation to them that he had not been shot.

Another man belonging to an Indiana regiment had a new pair of boots which he had refused to pull off the evening before. Next morning about sunrise a lieutenant with two sol-

diers and loaded muskets came to him and he was ordered to pull off the boots. He not complying immediately, the officer said: "You d—— rascal, pull off them boots or we will blow your brains out." The men seemed to be ready to carry the threat into execution and the man had to yield. I think if that lieutenant is ever caught out west by any of these boys they'll handle him rather rough. Once I was looking at one of the guards and thinking he was not the most intelligent specimen of humanity, he took from his pocket a whole ear of corn and commenced biting it off the cob like a hog, and continued to do so until the whole ear was devoured. Thinks I, if you are driven to such straits as that our chance for anything good to eat are not very flattering. During our stay here our number increased to 72, together with some seven or eight rebs who had been caught in the act of trying to desert. We represented seven states: New York, New Jersey, Pennsylvania, Ohio, Indiana, Illinois, Massachusetts, several from Ireland and two from Germany. At length came word to fall in, which order we could obey in short notice, not having much to encumber us we were marched to the depot and put into a box car, 11 o'clock at night. We found the place was terribly filthy, and on the morrow I found the car had been used in carrying mules and had never been cleaned out. In this place we were kept some 15 hours, at length stopping at a place called Corn Shops. We were permitted to get out and some of the men shoved the manure out of the car. At this place were long trains loaded with cotton and being run off ahead of General Sherman, who was after them with a long stick. I saw them giving the cotton away to any one who could manage to get off into the woods.

Then came the word that the Union Cavalry had cut the road in our part and we were ordered back to R (probably Raleigh) where we arrived in the middle of the night and marched to the old pen, arriving there we found everything deserted we were taken back to the depot to be ready for another move. Here we received word that Sherman's advance

guard was in the neighborhood and the town was being vacated by Johnson's army. Next day we started again on the railroad, this time putting us on top of the cars, all being filled to their utmost capacity. Thinking I might get pushed off the car I asked the guard the privilege of riding on a platform car which contained the brass pieces of artillery. On one of the guns I rode two days and one night. There were quite a number of their guns on the train and splendid ones they were. We had not proceeded many miles before we overtook Johnson's army, which we were several hours in passing. They were not marching on the railroad but on a parallel wagon road I could see them with their big guns stuck in the mud and the poor mules which were mostly skin and bones, receive terrible lashes because they were unable to draw them out. That day as we halted a few moments the guard saw a woman with a basket of cakes and pies for sale, he sent one of the men with rebel money to purchase some. The woman refused saying the money was not good, the man came back and made his report which threw the reb into a great rage, saying: "I'll learn her better than that," ordered two men to go and take from her the basket, which they did without giving the woman any compensation whatever. The history of the rebel money was a little curious. Travel fifty miles by rail and the money would pass without any trouble but it would take a basketful to buy a meal's victuals stay in that place two hours and you could find no one who would touch it. There came a boy with a few R—— papers, he asked ten cents Yankee money. "Haven't any I'll give you 50 cents confed. Don't want it. Why not. Because Sherman's at R——, and he'll knock the whole thing in the head. One of our men said I would like to have one of your papers but I haven't any Yankee money I will give you this Confed. dollar for one. The boy looked at him and said: "Well, take it." The boy took the money and then commenced tearing it up and throwing it on the ground. I said: "My boy, why do you do that?" He said; "It ain't worth ——— its gone up."

Previous to this there were rumors that Lee had surrendered, which was stoutly denied by the rebs. At length there came a man who had a paper giving an account of Lee's surrender, and commenced to read it to the guard. We were not slow in trying to gain a position where we could hear, and as he read on giving a somewhat detailed account of the surrender, our hearts swelled and it was with difficulty we could restrain our feelings and amid our privations that was a joyful day. Finally the course was clear, the road having been repaired, we were pushed on toward Salsbury which we had learned by this time was to be our final destination; arriving at Greensboro we were taken off the cars and for several days were marched from place to place, hardly staying twelve hours at any point. At length we set out on a march for Salisbury. We had not been more than an hour on our way when we received to us, the joyful news that General Stoneman was between us and that point. We were halted and soon retraced our steps to Greensboro. By this time Johnson's army began to arrive, we were put in a prison pen about a half mile from the town under a guard of eight and sometimes sixteen men. These men said they were heartily tired of the war and hoped it would soon be over so they could return to their families whom some of them had not seen for two years. Seeing they had no bayonets I inquired how it was, they said they were of no use and were thrown away more than a month ago. The truth was Sherman's men had given them a hint that they were not slow in taking. Sherman's men had adopted the plan of walking right up with charged bayonets and Johnny would be off in double quick, and so they came to the conclusion that bayonets were of no use. Their guns were rusty and everything betokened a disappointed and conquered people. There was nothing they had which looked like an army if you except the artillery. Their horses were mere skeletons; their wagons broken, many of them without any kind of cover; the best were mere shreads flying in the breeze, yet these were the paraphernalia with which they were going to conquer the great north.

Was there ever such stupendous folly? Jeff Davis passed through this place stopping a day or two in his flight south.

It was remembered he had been paying off the soldiers in specie; I saw one man who was paid off, he received $1.10 for two years service in the rebel army. We had been over two weeks getting here; had learned to lie down on the bare ground at night supperless and not complain, as that would have been useless. About this time we received the sad intelligence of the assination of President Lincoln. This was terrible; we tried to make ourselves believe it was a rebel canard, but alas it proved too true. I thought the rebs seemed to regret it quite as much as we did, saying Johnson would be harder on them than Lincoln. Now came news of an armistice between Sherman and Johnson, the terms of which were the south were to have their negroes and be restored to all their rights and privileges as before the rebellion. This was thought by some of our men to be glorious news. I told them if we did not have peace till we had it on those terms it would be long time coming. That the government would not accede to any such terms I was fully satisfied. The next news we heard on the subject was it had been rejected and Sherman was ordered forward. These were now anxious days and nights with us. We would lay and listen for Sherman's guns, hoping he would advance and give the rebs battle. Then came news of a new arrangement which proved more acceptable and was finally carried out. During all this time we were in a pitable condition; our clothing having become so dirty and filthy was not fit for human beings; no improvement in the rations except the better means of cooking. The boys by borrowing and taking as their own had managed to get some fair cooking utensils. Even then the one that was behind could not get his breakfast before 12 o'clock. Once in two or three days they would order us to fall in and march us through the town for what purpose we never did learn. Why they kept us at all was a mystery, as we seemed to be considerable trouble.

Johnson and Beaureguard had their headquarters in a

railroad car and would make speeches nearly every evening. We could hear the rebs cheering. One of our men being dangerously sick with the measels, the guard offered to get him a doctor. During the day one came, dressed in rebel uniform, went up to the man, looked at him as he lay on the ground and said: "Well, you have the measels, sure enough," and walked away. Some few of the men ran away. The boy Scott, of whom I spoke, was the first. He went off soon after we got to Greensboro. We expected he had got safely away, but the day we were liberated, who should come among us but Scott. He tried for two days and nights to get through the rebel pickets posted about four miles below us. He came very near being captured, and finally had to give it up. If he returned to the post he might be shot, so he went into the town and asked a negro for something to eat which was granted, with the offer of keeping him in his loft till such time as he could get away. Here he was kept and fed for two weeks. Two of the others got off and we never heard from them, so suppose they got safe through. These were anxious days with me, the days seemed long and weary; I was not sick, but was evidently losing my flesh so much so the men took notice of it. I seemed to have lost all relish for food. While the other men were suffering with hunger, I did not eat more than half that was dealt me. At last the time for our deliverance came Sunday, April 30th, 12 o'clock. Some of General Sherman's men finding us under rebel guard, told the guard to leave and we were free. Being permitted to walk out for the first time without a guard. I went to some negro quarters near by and asked for a cup of coffee; told them who I was, and how I came there. The kind hearted darkey woman said she had no coffee but if I would come back in about twenty minutes she would give me a cup of tea. I was back on time, and to my agreeable surprise found some excellent tea with milk and white sugar, warm wheat cakes, and fried ham. It seemed to me as if my appetite had been pent up for a month, and was now set free. I never tasted such tea and came to the conclusion that tea

was much better than coffee, and drank nothing else for six months afterward. The word had gone out and there was quite a number collected to see the Yankee prisoners. The negroes were from Virginia, having been run off here so that they could be taken back when the war was over. I asked them how they managed to get such good things to eat. The woman said that Massy was always looking out, but if there was anything to be had we know how to get it. They then began to question me about their being free. Said they had heard that Massa Lincoln would have set them free but he was killed and they were afraid they would still be slaves. I told them not to fear, for as soon as General Sherman came in and took charge, they would all be free. This gave them great encouragment, and they were the happiest creatures I ever saw. One old man said: "Oh bless de Lord; if I had wings I'd fly this minute." After partaking of this good meal, the first I had had for a month, I thanked them for their kindness and made my way back to the prison pen which was now near by we having been moved some three days previous. After we were liberated I went to the house of Mr. ——— who had formerly lived at Camden, N. J. He had visited us several times; said he was a Union man but was afraid to let his sentiment be known; remarking it would have cost him his life. At this time I wrote a letter to my family which reached them in five days. At 5 o'clock we started for R. (probably Raleigh) The night was stormy and being on a platform car the journey was not very pleasant, but the thought that I was free and on my way to my friends was enough. I could bear all inconveniences which seemed small compared with the prospect before me. We arrived at R——— about four o'clock in the morning. When it was light we saw the old United States flag floating over the rebel capital. I never saw it more glorious.

This day, May the first, we were put into comfortable quarters where we had a chance to wash and clean up. I spent part of the day in reflection and thankfulness to God who had protected and preserved me all the way through, and had

delivered me out of the hands of the rebels whose tenderest mercies are cruelty. That night we started for Newbern and arrived there about six P. M. the next day. As I was not subject to military duty or order, I was not long in finding my boarding house that I had left one month before. My friends did not recognize me and would have refused me admittance had I not made myself known. They were completely horror struck at my appearance. Could it be possible that such an object of pity was one they had ever known before? The women were soon alive to the severity of the case and I could see the tear start in the eyes as they looked at my pitable condition.

My nephew, Dr. D. W. Hand, was medical director of the post, having by chance heard of my return was soon with me and gave directions for my treatment. In a few days I was attacked with the scurvy and it was several weeks before I regained anything like my usual health.

THE TWO WAYS.

If I will force my way through briers, mud and the black
Black and mud will besmear me and the briers will scratch
back,
But if the prepared and open highway I will take
I'll pass easily along, and no commotion make.

So if I choose to travel with the bad and the wild,
The devil will see to it that I'm harrassed and riled,
While he who believes God and his prepared highway takes
Passes sweetly along like a boat on smooth lakes.

THE VICTORY SIDE.

In every conflict, every fight
Just ask which side is God's—the right,
And then you know which side will win,
Be it a year or be it ten.

That fact tells you which side to choose,
It also tells which side will lose,
Which side in time shall helped be
And sing the song of victory.

CHAPTER XXVI.

A ROMANCE.

At Cape May Court House north of the longest stream in Cape May County, Crooked Creek, at the southeast corner of the Ocean Boulevard and the Stone Harbor turnpike, are barns and sheds some of which are covered with the old dug-up shingles, and in others can be found the remains of a frame of large dimensions, perhaps 12x12 inches in width and thickness, yea, perhaps much larger, anyhow these buildings are the remains of an old home and additions thereto from one generation to another, from the time before Cape May was set off as a county (1692) until 1878, when it became the property of Mrs. Rebecca Ludlam and was sold by her heirs in 1909 to the brothers David, Reese P. and Howard Risley.

Two hundred years ago when some parts of these buildings formed the home of Cornelius Hand, Esq., they stood on the opposite side, i. e., at the southwest corner of the Stone Harbor branch of the Reading Railroad and Ocean Boulevard near where now stands the branch office of the South Jersey Realty Company. Here in this house was the First M. E. Church organization, consisting at first of twelve members, among them were Reuben Ludlam and Hannah his wife, Norton Ludlam and Judith his wife, and Mrs. Mary Yourison.

Very likely Mary Fifield (1803-1846) was another.

This was the beginning of the society that afterward built and worshipped in the old Ebenezer Church that stood where is now the M. E. cemetery and which society is today represented at the church that stands next to the County Court House on its north.

This Cornelius Hand had two charming daughters, Ruhama and Amelia. In this home of Cornelius Hand was once a large gathering, an assemblage of more than ordinary occurence. A wedding ceremony of a daughter of the aristocracy

of Middle Township to a son of the same of Dennis, is about to be performed. The smiling bride, Ruhama, dressed in her silk is ready; the groom with glowing pride stands waiting; the minister with the ritual open is present; all was gayety, charm and eager expectancy among the guests within.

But unknown to this company a sea captain has returned this very day to Beesley Point, N. J., the home of his parents, probably by the old slow stage coach of early days, or perhaps footsore from a long tramp, though he might have been set asore by some packet that entered great Egg Harbor. Anyhow he is soon told of the wedding announced to occur this evening, and though tired and wayworn he hastily robes himself in the best he at this time could command, procures a fast horse, springs into the saddle and rides in haste for Cape May Court House, likely down the old king's highway, hastening the steed with whip and spurs he nears the scene with but a few minutes to spare.

Hark, hark, what was that? A foam covered horse galloping furiously stops in front. Its rider, of beautiful face and fine physique, dismounts. He asks for the bride. She looks, she sees her first and former handsome lover who had sailed foreign seas and for years had been given up as dead, returned, alive, hearty and present. She rushes to his arms, entwines hers about his neck, they exchange words and kisses. He tells of gales, headwinds, mishaps, trading disasters and of shipwreck upon the Spanish main. The wedding is off as the bride, true to her first love, declares I'll not marry Henry; I'll not marry Henry; I'll not marry Henry. The commotion and excitement this evening and for days afterward is beyond me to describe, but as was the custom of that day, the minister then asked: "Is there anyone present who will marry Henry?" Whereupon a fine young lady of excellent family, Hannah Smith by name, replied: "I'll marry Henry; I'll marry Henry; Henry I'll marry thee. And Henry replied "I'll marry thee, Hannah. So upon the evening of February 11, 1771, Ruhama Hand married the young sea captain Nicholas Still-

well and not Henry Ludlam, but the noble-souled gentleman that he proved himself to be to the end of his life (1752 to 1837) acted the part of bridegroom and Miss Hannah Smith was bridesmaid, but Henry was so wounded that not until June 30th, 1772, did he consent to allow the wedding ceremony that made Hannah his wife to take place.

Both marriages proved to be most excellent matches and many of their descendants of today are of the very best of Middle, Dennis and Upper Townships families, and if I mistake not some are in Lower Township, while others may be found living far, far, away from said scene. In after years the children of Hannah tell how near they came to being the children of Ruhama, or, in other words, how near X came to being Z, or Z came to being X.

For the benefit of descendants we append the following: John Hand of Kent County, England, was in Southampton as early as 1644. His son Shamgar, settled at Cape May Court House about 1690, next in line likely comes Jeremiah Hand, Esq., whose son Cornelius Hand was the father of Ruhama, who married Capt. Nicholas Stillwell, and also of Amelia Hand, who married John Ludlam, whose sons were Norton and Reuben.

Nicholas and Ruhama's daughter Jane married Daniel Whilden and left Amelia, Alexander and Danelia. Amelia became the wife of Samuel Springer. Danelia became the wife of Franklin Hand. Ruhama when a widow married Matthew Whilden.

Of the other family Esq. Henry Ludlam, Sr., was a son of Joseph II, grandson of Joseph I. Hannah was the daughter of Daniel Smith, tea merchant and trader with many countries, and today there are China cups, saucers, punch bowl, etc., in the families of this line which were brought from China and ports of other countries.

Henry Ludlam, Esq., and Hannah Smith left Abigail, who married Joseph Falkinburge, who after her death married her sister Sarah. Abigail left Abigail, who married Jeremiah

Leaming, leaving the Hon. Richard S. Leaming. Daniel. Henry Ludlam, Jr., who married Mary Lawrence (daughter of James and Sarah). Joseph, who left Joseph and Isabel, who married Lewis Leaming. James married Jane Ritchie. Lewis married Jane Swayne. Hannah. Richard Smith Ludlam that married Ellen Hughes

Henry Ludlam, Jr., and Mary Lawrence's children were: Hannah S. Ludlam, who married William S. Townsend. Maria. Abigail F. Ludlam, who married George B. Stratton. Sarah Ann Ludlam , who married Humphrey Leaming. Eleanor Hughes Ludlam. Henry. Albert Henry Ludlam, who married Elizabeth Champion. Emeline. Joseph May Ludlam, who married Isabel Holmes, a daughter of Nathaniel.

My Second Book

South Jersey Spray

Is in Preparation

Parties having stories of State, County, Village or Family History or accounts and views of noted sights, might get them published if forwarded to

CHARLES TOMLIN

CAPE MAY COURT HOUSE, NEW JERSEY

SAVIR

A Device That Saves One-Half Your Coal

Cost You Nothing to Prove It.

WHAT IT WILL DO

Saves half of your Coal, Wood or Coke.

Saves labor in handling of fuel and ashes. No clinkers.

Produces steady, lasting fires without constant watching.

Increases hot water supply.

Gives hotter ovens.

Saves life—no fatal gases in the house. No over-heated flues.

Lasts as long as your range.

Brings happiness to the cook.

Pays for itself in the use of two tons of coal.

TRY IT FOR ONE WEEK FREE OF CHARGE

PRE-HEATED AIR CO.

SAVIR

FUEL SAVING DEVICES

Suite 628-629-630

1011 Chestnut Street **Philadelphia, Pa.**

Bell Phone, Walnut 4477

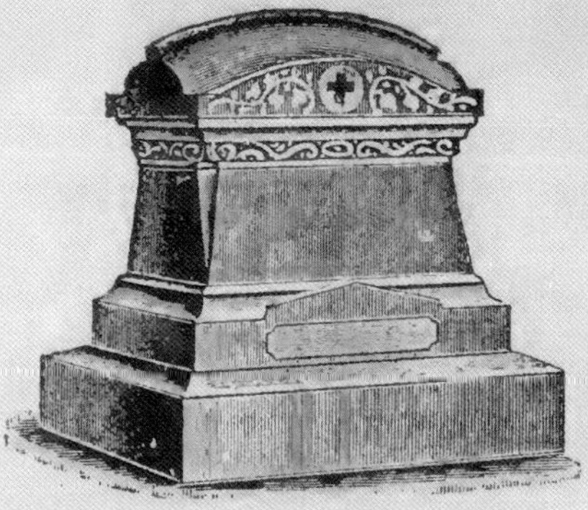

I Make Every Customer My Friend

Wm. F. Daniels

Manufacture aud Dealer in

Granite and Marble Work

Drop a postal or phone

Cape May Court House :: New Jersey

Walter Hurrell

Manufacturer and Dealer in

All Kinds of **HARNESS**

Lap Robes, Blankets, Whips, Etc.

Repairing a Specialty

South Main Street
Cape May Court House, N. J.

EDWIN Z. MILLS

House and Sign

PAINTING

PAPER HANGING

Cape May Court House
New Jersey

R. M. ELMER

Bread Cake and Pie Bakery

Cape May Court House, N. J.

Marula

An imprint of Arcadia Publishing

Cape May Spray
by Charles Tomlin

A Marula Historical Reprint
Originally published in 1899

Published by Arcadia Publishing
Charleston SC

ISBN 978-0-7385-9452-1

Printed in the United States of America

For all general information contact Arcadia Publishing at:
Telephone 843-853-2070
Fax 843-853-0044
E-mail sales@arcadiapublishing.com
For customer service and orders:
Toll-Free 1-888-313-2665

Visit us on the Internet at www.arcadiapublishing.com

Cape May Spray

By Charles Tomlin